The Scien[tific] Method in Fairy Tale Forest

By Laura Magner

Pieces of Learning

© 2007 Pieces of Learning
CLC0405
ISBN 978-1-931334-94-5
Graphic Production by Sharolyn Hill
www.piecesoflearning.com

Contents

The Scientific Method in Fairy Tale Forest

I want students to be more than learners. I want them to be questioners. I want them to be keen observers of their environment, continually generating their own questions about the world and how it works.

Then I want them to actively find the answers to their questions. I want them to think across the curriculum, making connections and not departmentalizing their thinking.

While reading to my children at bedtime, I started to see great teaching points in their stories – places in the text that made me momentarily forget the story and think about *what ifs*. I thought about tie-ins to math, and I thought about testing some story elements scientifically.

Could a wolf *really* blow down a straw house?
Should Baby Bear's porridge *really* be the one that was just right?
Can one night of dancing *really* wear out a pair of shoes?
Could Hansel and Gretel *really* follow some shiny pebbles all the way home?

As you read the fairy tales used in this book and enjoy the familiar stories start thinking about all the possibilities for extensions. A few scientific questions have been pulled out, but you may very well think of more. For each fairy tale are suggestions for research and math extensions to take the questioning even further.

In this book, science will be explored in the following areas:
Earth Science - the sun, weather, light energy
Health Science - anatomy, criminology, human observation
Life Science - ecology, animals, biology, plants and life cycles,
Physical Science - chemistry, chemical change, physical change,
                    matter, physics, friction

The Scientific Method

The Scientific Method is necessary to scientific discovery. Since the days of Galileo, men and women have been following the five familiar steps to try to explain their questions about the world around them. Several variations can be found on the exact steps, sub-steps and inclusions in the Scientific Method. Plus, there is variation in the Method depending on the type of experiments being considered.

In physical science, data is collected in the form of numbers and measurable changes in particles or forces. If the experiments are in descriptive science like life sciences, animals or people-data is more likely taken from observation or interviews.

This book uses fairy tales as a context to practicing the scientific method and learning scientific knowledge. Many of the activities do not strictly follow all five steps as you would in true lab experiments. But they do involve the spirit of all five steps. Because the questions are derived from the fairy tales, the initial question is mine, and then handed over to the students. Below is a description of the **Scientific Method**.

1. **Initial Observation**: you notice, you wonder, you ask questions. Make a purpose statement during this step. What do you want to find out? Also, identify any variables that may affect the experiment.
2. **Make a Hypothesis**: This is a question that has been re-worded and expresses a cause and effect relationship. It's an educated guess that seeks to possibly explain your question.
3. **Make Predictions and Design an Experiment** to test your hypothesis. Usually a "control" is used. Select one thing that will be changed. This is the *variable*.
4. **Test your Hypothesis**. Many times, experiments are repeated several times to verify that the researcher got a true, reproducible result. Keep careful notes.
5. **Draw a Conclusion** about the hypothesis. Summarize the results and report. Were there any difficulties? What would you change or do differently? What did you learn?

So, OBSERVE and QUESTION, GUESS, PLAN, DO and REPORT.

The Scientific Method is a wonderful skill to possess. It has uses beyond the area of science. Once children are practiced in conducting experiments in science, they can move to solving real life problems with the Method. The phone doesn't work. Why? Use a hypothesis. *The phone doesn't work because the batteries are dead.* Test it out! Your baby sister is upset. Make a hypothesis. *My baby sister is upset because she needs to eat something.* Test it out! Was it food, or was it clean clothes or a nap?

The Scientific Method

Support for Hands-On Science and Cross-Curricular Activities

The NSTA's (National Science Teachers Association) position on teaching science in the elementary school is that all students of all learning levels participate in science inquiry and hands-on science activities. In fact, the NSTA suggests that of the time spent teaching science to young children, 60% of it should be hands-on (Position Statement.)

The National Science Education Standards, Teaching Standard B summarizes almost a mirror image to the scientific method. In order to do scientific inquiry, students need to
*Ask a question (about objects, organisms, and events in the environment,
*Plan and conduct a simple investigation,
*Employ simple equipment and tools to gather data and extend the senses,
*Use data to construct a reasonable explanation, and
*Communicate investigations and explanations. (Content Standards K-4)

The Scientific Method in Fairy Tale Forest combines reading instruction with science, and therefore **curiosity, critical thinking, inquiry, data collection** and **written expression**. Research shows that practice using **cooperative learning**, **summarizing and note taking**, and **generating and testing hypotheses** will result in significant gains in student achievement (Marzano, et al.)

The Scientific Method in Fairy Tale Forest will give your students practice in both inductive and deductive experiments. Each lesson cites the classic fairy tale from which the lesson ideas were inspired. Then a **science spark** is given, which is the guiding question from the fairy tale, and the experiment is outlined. The activities will get young students familiar with the Scientific Method, asking them to **make a hypothesis** that correlates with the questions posed, conduct an organized experiment, keep detailed records and draw conclusions. On the teacher page, background information for explaining the expected outcome of the experiment is given. A materials list is provided to assist the teacher in lesson set-up. Every effort has been made to create experiments that use common inexpensive materials that are readily available to teachers.

Utilizing the Lessons

Activities from The Scientific Method in Fairy Tale Forest can be incorporated into thematic units already in use in your classroom, choosing the fairy tales that are already part of your curriculum. Or choose a less familiar tale that ties in and is appropriate. Teachers may also use the table of contents to choose a scientific principle being studied in their science text, and thereby tie in literature for an overlapping, whole approach.

The Scientific Method

Assessing the Lessons

The Scientific Method in Fairy Tale Forest activities are in a way their own assessment of student scientific knowledge. The lessons model a scientific way of thinking and allow for student review of each other's work, find mistakes in their processes, identify faulty reasoning and amend their conclusions. There need not be a test later. The way the students handle the activities and the scientific method is an assessment in itself. Students will learn self-assessment and will become more confident in their abilities to *do* science through these fun activities.

Science Clubs

Lessons from *The Scientific Method in Fairy Tale Forest* are also excellent for science clubs. My school has an All Girls Science Club made up of third through fifth grade girls. The club meets once a week in the morning before school, conducting different experiments and exploring topics – everything from recycling to the dissolved oxygen content of the water in the stream that runs along our school's property. Our science specialist teacher is the creator and facilitator of the group, and she has graciously invited me in several times to test out some lessons with her girls.

This club is an excellent chance to bring in the opportunity for new science learning, touching on concepts that may not be addressed in science texts. Fairy tales may be assigned as outside reading in preparation for the next week's club meeting. Then, the instructor can simply review key points in the tale and move right on to the days' experiment. Since the tales included here spark several questions and experiments, one tale could provide a month's worth of club lessons.

Thinking continues at home with I WONDER cards

The goal of these lessons, as stated before, is two-fold. Teach and allow students to become fluent in the scientific method. The other goal is to encourage them and model for them how to notice the possibility for testing scientific principles in lots of places. Science doesn't happen only in *science class*. Show them the excitement in asking and finding the answers to their own questions. Give your students a simple index card with the words I WONDER written on the top. Encourage them to use this I WONDER card as a bookmark. As they read on their own they should write down questions they have as they read. Record questions that they feel might be answered through scientific inquiry. Periodically ask the students to share their I WONDER questions and choose a few to test in class. Turn the attention to nursery rhymes and popular chapter books as well. *What would really happen if a big egg fell off of a wall?* (Humpty Dumpty) *Can you make a chocolate frog?* (Harry Potter)

Little Red Riding Hood
OVERVIEW

Story version used: classic retelling by Scott Gustafson

Little Red Riding Hood #1

 Science Spark What flora and fauna are right outside your classroom door?
Science Area/Principle Life Science, Ecology and Animals
The Lesson Students will hypothesize about what species of plants and animals live on their school grounds. They will then use their senses while outside to discover and record who and what they sense living at school.

Little Red Riding Hood #2

Science Spark How much food can your stomach hold?
Science Area/Principle Health Science, Anatomy
The Lesson Students will hypothesize about the size of their stomachs. Using a balloon and sand, students will experiment with stretching their model stomach to see how much it can hold.

 ## Research Extensions

The wolf had gone three days without food.
What effect would three days without food have on wolves or other mammals?
Find out what wolves eat, how often they eat, and if they could go three days without food.

The hunter heard the wolf snoring.
Some people snore and some do not. What causes some people to snore? Look up snoring. Are there ways to prevent it? Does anyone in your house snore?

Math Extensions

Red Riding Hood walks a half hour to get to her grandma's house.
How far can you walk in a half hour? Would the distance be different for an adult than it would be for a child? Why or why not? Go outside and walk for 5 minutes. Measure the distance you traveled. Multiply by six to see how far you could probably go in a half hour.

Little Red Riding Hood
BACKGROUND INFORMATION

Little Red Riding Hood #1

Science Spark __What flora and fauna are right outside your classroom door?__

Science Area/Principle Life Science, Ecology and Animals

Additional Materials Needed Clipboards, digital camera, and portable tape recorder to take outside (optional)

The Lesson

Set It Up
Read the classic version of Little Red Riding Hood. Talk about Red Riding Hood's walk through the woods on her way to her grandmother's house. **What would she have seen and smelled in the woods?**

Discuss the science spark. Ask students to **make a hypothesis** about what plants and animals they would see, hear, and smell on school grounds and record them on their activity pages. Discuss your school campus with the class. Decide together where the best place would be to observe plants and animals.

Divide the students into three groups. Inform each group what their focus will be once outside: One group will observe and record sights; one group will observe and record sounds; and one group will observe and record smells. Students may want to take a clipboard with them so it is easier to record their observations on their activity sheets.

Conduct the Experiment
Take the class outside to the appropriate area. You may want to give the students a time limit, and encourage them to be silent for that period of time while they observe. Have them record what their senses detect outside. Ask them to focus only on their assigned sense.

Wrap It Up/Expected Outcomes
Once back in the classroom, have the students share what they recorded. Students should make conclusions based on their outside experiences, and record them on their sheets. What students observe will vary, depending on your school's location. Check for logical answers.

Continue the discussion. (*How similar do you think the woods that Little Red Riding Hood was in is to the school grounds? Would she have seen, heard, and smelled what we just did?*) Remind students that this classic fairy tale most likely originated in Europe. *Are their wooded areas similar to ours?*

Little Red Riding Hood #1

The wolf tells Little Red Riding Hood to stop and look around her and notice the beauty of the woods.

What would you see if you went outside and stopped to take a look and listen to the world around you?

Is there natural beauty at your school?

Science Spark What flora and fauna are right outside your classroom door?

Make a hypothesis: Make a statement that you think explains what plants and animals live in your school environment. What do you expect to see, hear, and/or smell?

My hypothesis:

Little Red Riding Hood #1

Now you will work in small groups to stop and observe nature right outside your classroom door. Assist your teacher in deciding what spot is best on your school grounds to observe nature.

Your teacher will put you into groups. Take paper and a pencil to keep careful notes. In the time allowed, <u>use words and drawings</u> to record what you observe.

You will be in one of the following groups: What **sounds** are outside? What **sights** are outside? What **smells** are outside?

Record your observations of the school's natural environment below.

I am in the group that (circle one) listens looks smells

Report and reflect on your findings. Was your hypothesis correct? Were you surprised by anything you observed outside? Describe your conclusions.

How would this observation experiment differ if it were dusk, or dark, or dawn?

Little Red Riding Hood
BACKGROUND INFORMATION

Little Red Riding Hood #2

Science Spark How much food can your stomach hold?

Science Area/Principle Health Science, Anatomy

Additional Materials Needed

One 4"-5" deflated balloon per small group, approximately one gallon of sand, birdseed, or other similar granular material, plastic or hand made cardboard funnels, plastic spoons, one previously prepared 'child sized' stomach containing about 1 liter of sand

The Lesson

Set It Up

Read the classic version of Little Red Riding Hood. The wolf ate the grandmother *and* Little Red Riding Hood! How could he do that? Is that possible? How big is a wolf's stomach or a human's stomach?

Have students **make a hypothesis** about how much food they think their stomachs could hold. Encourage them to use actual measurements in their statements, such as 1 cup, 2 cups, etc.

Conduct the Experiment

Read together the background information given on the activity sheet. Review the directions for the activity. Students will be given balloons that represent the actual size of their stomachs. They will use funnels to help fill the balloons with as much 'food' as they think a real stomach could actually hold.

When they think they have stretched it far enough, assist them in tying the balloon. Students then need to measure the balloon width and record it on their sheets.

When all groups are finished, they will share the widths of their balloons, and all students will record their classmates' answers on their sheets.

Wrap It Up/ Expected Outcomes

Student balloon 'stomachs' will vary, but will most likely contain .5 liter of sand (____cups).

Share with the students a balloon that you have previously prepared.
Some sources report that the human stomach can actually stretch 50 times its empty volume! An 'adult' sized balloon could then contain as much as 2-3 liters. Your 'child sized' balloon should contain about *one liter of sand! (___ cups)*

Allow students to share their reactions to the amazingly stretchy human stomach. After seeing the model 'stomach,' they need to record their conclusions on the bottom of their activity sheets.

Little Red Riding Hood #2

The wolf swallowed the grandmother and Little Red Riding Hood.

How big is the average stomach? How much can it stretch?

 **How much food can your stomach hold?**

Make a hypothesis: Make a statement that explains how far you think your stomach could stretch. How flexible is it?

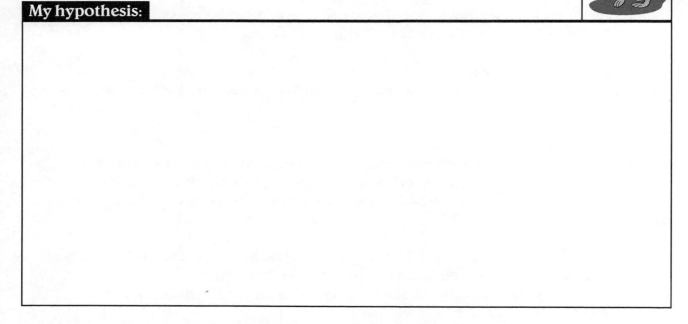

My hypothesis:

Your stomach is a muscular sac shaped like the letter J. It is very flexible. In this activity you will try to see just how much a stomach can stretch each time you eat!

An adult stomach is about 25 cm long. Your stomach is probably a third of that size, or about 8–10 cm long. When the stomach is empty, the space inside is about 0.08 liters. Your teacher will give you and a partner a balloon. Measure the balloon's width. Is it 8-10 cm? It's just like your empty stomach! How far do you think your stomach will stretch? Let's see!

1. Stretch the end of the balloon over the end of the funnel.
2. Hold the neck of the balloon where it meets the funnel. Hold the funnel upright.

Little Red Riding Hood #2

3. Spoon sand into the funnel a little bit at a time. With a free hand, stretch the balloon and move the sand around so more can fit in (but don't let go of the balloon's neck.)

4. Keep adding sand until you think you have stretched the balloon as far as your stomach could actually stretch. When you decide to stop, ask your teacher to tie the top of the balloon in a knot.

Measure your balloon's width. **We think our stomach would stretch to _____cm.**

Listen as your classmates share how far they stretched their balloons. Record some of their measurements:

Group member names	length of balloon in cm amount of sand in cups
	_____
	_____
	_____
	_____
	_____
	_____

Watch as your teacher shows you just how far the stomach **can** actually stretch.

Report and reflect on your findings. Was your hypothesis correct? Were you surprised by how much a stomach can stretch? Describe your conclusions on another sheet of paper.

Snow White and the Seven Dwarfs*
OVERVIEW

Story version used: classic retelling by Scott Gustafson
Classic spelling of *dwarfs

Snow White and the Seven Dwarfs #1

Science Spark How observant are you?
Science Area/Principle Health Science, Criminology, and Observation
The Lesson Students will hypothesize about how well they observe and whether or not they would be a good eyewitness. They will test their hypothesis when they observe a 'crime' and have to record their observations and check for accuracy.

Snow White and the Seven Dwarfs #2

Science Spark How would adding a poison to a fruit affect its appearance?
Science Area/Principle Physical Science, Chemistry, Chemical vs. Physical Change
The Lesson Students will hypothesize about how a poison would change a fruit. The teacher will inject an apple with bleach, and students will observe it over time to see if the poison affects its appearance.

Snow White and the Seven Dwarfs #3

Science Spark What will happen to an organic item when it is sealed in glass or plastic?
Science Area/Principle Life Science, Biology, and Ecology
The Lesson Students will make a hypothesis to explain what happens when a food is encased in an airtight container. The students will place a mashed, ripe fruit or vegetable in a capped water bottle and observe it over several days.

Research Extensions

The hunter returned with a baby bear's heart instead of Snow White's heart.
What is the difference between a human heart and a bear heart?

The men mined iron and gold.
How are these metals mined, and what do they look like in their raw form?

Math Extensions

Find out the current value of an ounce of iron and gold.

Snow White took one sip from each cup hoping the dwarfs wouldn't notice that she had some of their drinks.
How much liquid is in an average sip? Measure it.

Snow White and the Seven Dwarfs
BACKGROUND INFORMATION

Snow White and the Seven Dwarfs #1

Science Spark How observant are you?

Science Area/Principle Health Science, Criminology and Observation

Additional Materials Needed Prop purse, briefcase, cell phone, etc.

**Before the lesson Rearrange or remove small items in your classroom – nothing extensive – but something that only the most observant students would notice. Next, either pull two to three students out ahead of time, and enlist them in a 'crime drama' scenario skit, or utilize students from another class (preferred method.) Briefly go over what the 'actors' should do and say. The goal is that they will be unobtrusive. You want to see which students notice pertinent information, so the 'crime' should not be blatant. Students can come in to borrow a book or other item. They can then take a valuable item like purse or cell phone (props) that may or may not be in a drawer. The incident should be quick, and they may or may not want to use names while they commit the crime.

The Lesson

Set It Up
At the start of the lesson, read Snow White and talk about how the dwarfs knew that someone had been in the house. Would the students notice such a thing at their houses?

Have students **make a hypothesis** about how well they think they observe what's around them. Once these are recorded, tell students that some things in the classroom have been moved. Can they find them? Have them list them on their activity sheets.

Conduct the Experiment
This takes timing: While students are recording what they observe have been moved, direct your 'actors' to enter the room. Sneakily, the actors need to borrow a book, take your 'purse' (or other prop) and then leave.

Ask the students: _What just happened? Did you see that?_ Have them describe what they noticed happening, trying to include information that would be helpful in solving the 'crime.' (*How many intruders were there? How tall were they? What were they wearing? Did they say anything? What did they take? What did that item look like? Which person was the one who actually picked it up?*)

Wrap It Up/Expected Outcomes
Allow students to share aloud their versions of what just happened. (You may want to request that they not change their account of the 'crime' as other students start to share information. They should be decisive and stick to their recollections of the incident.) Some students may

Snow White and the Seven Dwarfs
BACKGROUND INFORMATION

Snow White and the Seven Dwarfs #1

remember what one person wore, but not the other. They may remember hair color, but may not be able to provide other facial information.

After most students have shared their versions, you may tell them the factual 'crime scenario' information. If the 'actors' could come back in and stand before the group, your students could compare their notes and memory of sizes, colors etc. to the real people.

Also, share with the students what classroom item or items were moved.

After hearing the recap, students need to draw conclusions about how observant they are based on the two opportunities for practice that they just had.

Snow White and the Seven Dwarfs #1

The dwarfs return from work and can tell that someone had been in their house.

Would you be able to tell if someone had been in the room before you? Would you make a good detective? Would you make a good eyewitness?

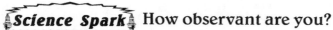 **Science Spark** How observant are you?

Make a hypothesis: Make a statement that explains how observant you are; how well do you notice what is around you?

My hypothesis:

Detectives and police officers often have to depend on eyewitnesses to help them solve cases. Would you make a good eyewitness? How good is your memory of your classroom, and how well have you paid attention today?

Before you came in, your teacher made some changes to the everyday set up of the room! Look around. See what the classroom usually looks like in your *mind's eye*. Notice any differences? List them on another sheet of paper.

Snow White and the Seven Dwarfs #1

What just happened? Did you see that?   How well did you pay attention to important details? Are you as observant as the dwarfs were?

What did you hear and see? Describe the scene you just observed. Summarize, and only include what you think are the most important details. Include descriptions of colors, sizes, and sounds.

After hearing a recap of the events by the teacher, how well did your hypothesis hold up?

Describe your accuracy, what you learned, and what you might do differently next time if you were ever called upon to be an eyewitness!
Write your conclusions below.

Snow White and the Seven Dwarfs
BACKGROUND INFORMATION

Snow White and the Seven Dwarfs #2

Science Spark How would adding poison to a fruit affect its appearance?

Science Area/Principle Physical Science, Chemistry, Chemical vs. Physical Change

Additional Materials Needed

Three apples, bleach, rubbing alcohol*, two syringes, three paper plates, three small stickers, rubber gloves, well ventilated area   *or choose another suitable liquid

The Lesson

Set It Up

Read Snow White. Discuss how the witch poisoned the apple that caused Snow White to sleep. Wouldn't Snow White notice the apple had been tampered with? Have the students **make a hypothesis** about how a poison may affect a fruit.

Today you will be injecting two 'poisons' into apples in order for the students to observe what happens. One apple will remain a *control*. ONLY the teacher should touch the bleach and rubbing alcohol and syringes. Students are to OBSERVE only from a safe distance and should never touch the apples once the toxins have been added.

Conduct the Experiment

Have students assist in setting up the experiment. They will place an apple in the center of each plate. Label plates – #1, #2, #3, and place a sticker on the side of each apple. The sticker will mark the spot where the 'poison' will be added.

With students gathered around, explain the purpose of the *control* apple. Ask a student to label the #1 paper plate with the word *control*. Carefully prepare each syringe, and inject the other liquids into the apples. Students should observe from a safe distance for a few moments, and then record what they see happening to each apple.

Students will again return to observe, and then record, what they see after 30 minutes and then after several hours. Then, while wearing rubber gloves, cut each apple near the sticker/ poison site, and observe the inside in order to see any differences in the flesh.

Wrap It Up/Expected Outcomes

Likely outcomes are as follows:

	first injection	*30 minutes*	*after a few hours*	*flesh inside*
Apple #1	N/A	No change	No change	Unaffected
Apple #2 bleach	No real change seen	Injection hole seems bigger	No change	Flesh is mushy and whiter at the site
Apple #3 alcohol	No real change seen	Area around hole looks bruised	Flesh inside injection hole is brown	Flesh is brown about 1cm around the site

Discuss the experiment. Have students record their conclusions and answer the questions.

Snow White and the Seven Dwarfs #2

The stepmother takes an apple and makes the rosy, appealing side poisonous.

Would you be able to tell if a fruit had had poison injected into it? Would the poison stay to one side of an apple, or would it spread to the whole fruit?

Science Spark How would adding poison to a fruit affect its appearance?

Make a hypothesis: Make a statement that you think explains what effect poison would have on a piece of raw fruit.

My hypothesis:

Follow the directions below to conduct an experiment to see what would really happen if someone tried to infect a fruit with a poison.

You need three apples. One apple will not have any poison added to it. It is your **control** apple. The other apples will each have a different *poison* added to them. The poisons used in the experiment are <u>bleach</u> and <u>rubbing alcohol</u>. <u>ONLY your teacher should handle these liquids</u>. Your job is to **observe**.

Your teacher will ask for your help. Each apple needs to be placed in the center of a paper or Styrofoam plate. Label the control apple #1, then the next apple #2, and the next #3. Place a small sticker on one side of each apple. This is the spot where the poison will be injected. Watch as your teacher injects the *poison* into the flesh of the apples.

Snow White and the Seven Dwarfs #2

Record what happens immediately after the poisons are added. Record the time as well:

	liquid	*time*	*reaction*
Apple #1	control	_____	_____
Apple #2	bleach	_____	_____
Apple #3	rubbing alcohol	_____	_____

After 30 minutes, <u>look closely</u> at the apples again. DO NOT TOUCH them. Note any differences in the fruits. Be sure you compare the side with the sticker (the site of the poison) with the other areas of the fruit. Record your observations below.

Apple #1 _____

Apple #2 _____

Apple #3 _____

Snow White's stepmother made the poisonous apple and then headed for the dwarfs' house that day. So the poison would be in the apple for less than a day. Let the apples sit, and come back in a few hours to check on them. Do not touch the apples.

After a few hours have passed, reexamine the three apples to see if they look any different. Does the poison seem to have made any changes in the apples' appearance? Describe below what you observe.

Apple #1 _____

Apple #2 _____

Apple #3 _____

What about the inside of the apples? Has the poison affected the flesh of the apple? Would Snow White have noticed anything when she bit into the poisonous apple?

Snow White and the Seven Dwarfs #2

Watch and record what you observe as your teacher cuts the apples at the poison site.

Apple #1 _____

Apple #2 _____

Apple #3 _____

Look back at your hypothesis. Think about what you have observed with the apples. Summarize your conclusions below. What did you learn about poison and fruit?

Do you think other fruits would have the same reaction to poisons being added to them? If so, what fruits would be similar to the apple?

What fruits do you think would have a different reaction to the poison? why?

What about other foods? What foods do you think would change due to poison being added to them? Why do you think that?

Snow White and the Seven Dwarfs
BACKGROUND INFORMATION

Snow White and the Seven Dwarfs #3

Science Spark __What happens to an organic item when sealed in glass or plastic?__

Science Area/Principle Life Science, Biology, Ecology

Additional Materials Needed

Three empty, clean, and dry water bottles or glass bottles, one fruit sample, one vegetable sample, and a small leaf bundle per group, three balloons, three paper plates or pieces of wax paper, three plastic spoons, permanent marking pen, plastic tape. These should be multiplied accordingly if several groups will do all three bottles.

TheLesson

Set It Up

Read or remind students about the story ending of Snow White. The dwarfs placed Snow White in a glass coffin in the woods where she remained unchanged for a long period of time until the prince found her. What would really happen if you placed something that had once been living into a closed container? Have the students **make a hypothesis** on their papers.

Conduct the Experiment

Divide the students into three groups. Divide the materials so each group has one bottle, either a fruit piece, a vegetable piece, or the leaves. Each group will do the following:

⇨ Use a plastic spoon to mash the 'living' sample.
⇨ Carefully spoon the mash into the bottle.
⇨ Use the pen to write the name of the plant and the day's date on the bottle. Also, they should make a horizontal line that shows the top edge of the mash inside the bottle.
⇨ One group member will hold the bottle while another carefully stretches a balloon over the mouth of the bottle. Pull the balloon down at least an inch over the bottle treads.
⇨ Plastic tape will seal the connection between the balloon and the bottle.

Line up the bottles in a location where all the students can observe them. They need to record what the plants look like now, including information about the color and texture of the contents.

Leave them for 24 hours. Again, have students observe the mash, and record what they observe happening.

Check on the bottles each day for 4-5 days. After 4-5 days, have students record what happened to the organic material.

Snow White and the Seven Dwarfs
BACKGROUND INFORMATION

Snow White and the Seven Dwarfs #3

Wrap it Up/Expected Outcomes

After viewing the plant samples, they should summarize their conclusions about what would *really* have happened to Snow White if she had been sealed in an airtight glass coffin.

What will happen: The plant mash in the bottles will begin to be decomposed by bacteria that were already present in the material. As the bacteria attack the mash, gas is released. Over a few days, the gas will collect in the bottle and eventually inflate the balloon enough that the balloon should stick straight up. (It will not inflate and stretch as much as it would if it was blown up, but it should fill and lift itself upright.) The more liquid in your fruit and vegetable samples, the faster the experiment will work. (I used half a nectarine, and in three days, the balloon was upright.) Also, the more a sample is touched by humans, the more bacteria will be present, especially if the food was half eaten and picked up bacteria from a mouth! Sunlight seems to speed the process.

Snow White and the Seven Dwarfs #3

The dwarfs put Snow White in a glass coffin where she stayed for years and years until the prince found her in perfect condition!

Can you leave any once living thing in glass for years and years without them changing? How long can you leave it there?

Science Spark **What happens to an organic item when sealed in glass or plastic?**

Make a hypothesis: Make a statement that tells what you think what would happen to an organic item once it was sealed airtight.

My hypothesis:

You will be conducting an experiment to see what happens to plants when they are sealed in an airtight container.

Take the fruit, vegetable, or leaves that your teacher provides you. On the paper plate:

⇨ Use a plastic spoon to mash your plant sample.

⇨ Carefully spoon the mash into the bottle.

⇨ Use the pen to write the name of the plant and today's date on the bottle. Also, make a horizontal line that shows how high up the mash is inside the bottle.

⇨ Have one group member hold the bottle while another carefully stretches a balloon over the mouth of the bottle. Pull the balloon down at least an inch.

⇨ Take some plastic tape to seal the balloon to the bottle.

Snow White and the Seven Dwarfs #3

Describe below each of the plants being used in your experiment. What do they look like inside the bottles? What is their color, texture?

Bottle #1
Fruit:

Bottle #2
Vegetable:

Bottle #3
Leaves:

Come back in 24 hours to check on it. What are the changes you can see? Are the colors the same? Do they still fill the bottle to the same point as before? Record what you see.

Bottle #1

Bottle #2

Bottle #3

Check on the bottles each day for up to a week. What is happening to the organic material?

Summarize your conclusions about what happens to organic material when left in an airtight container over time. What did you learn?

Tom Thumb
OVERVIEW

Story version used: classic retelling by Scott Gustafson

Tom Thumb #1

Science Spark What would happen to a leaf hat over time?
Science Area/Principle Life Science, Plants and Life Cycles
The Lesson Students will hypothesize and experiment about what happens to leaves when they are picked from a tree and no longer have that connection to nutrients.

Tom Thumb #2

Science Spark What happens to batter when it is boiled?
Science Area/Principle Physical Science, Chemistry, Matter
The Lesson Students will hypothesize about what actually happens in foods when they are boiled. The class will make a 'cloutie' (boiled pudding) as decribed in the story in order to observe how food changes form.

Tom Thumb #3

Science Spark Are you nearsighted?
Science Area/Principle Health Science, Anatomy
The Lesson Students will hypothesize about how well they see with their eyes. They will then participate in various sight tests to see how well they see with their right and left eye sand gain experiences about what farsighted and nearsighted means.

 ## Research Extensions

A nearsighted hawk mistook Tom for a toad.
What food do hawks prefer? Do they really like toads?

Birds follow the plow looking for grubs.
What is a grub? Do birds feed primarily on grubs? How does a plow work? How would it unearth grubs?

 ## Math Extensions

Tom can bathe in a coffee mug, ride a mouse, or fit in a pocket.
Figure out the scale. What percentage of an average child is Tom?

Tom Thumb
BACKGROUND INFORMATION

Tom Thumb #1

Science Spark __What happens to a leaf hat over time?__

Science Area/Principle Life Science, Plants, and Life Cycles

Additional Materials Needed

Several freshly picked leaves – oak, and two other kinds, enough for each group to have what they need to make small hats, a variety of fasteners like pins, pipe cleaners, staples, tape, wax paper as a work surface, small dolls or small stuffed animals to model the hats! (Can be provided by students)

The Lesson

Set It Up

Read Tom Thumb. Talk about the outfit that was made just for him. The hat was made from oak leaves. Would a hat made of oak leaves stay nice and keep its shape for a long time? Have students **make a hypothesis** about what they think will happen over time to a hat made of leaves.

Tell the students that they will be making small hats like the one Tom Thumb had. Have them record on their activity sheets the three kinds of leaves they will use.

Conduct the Experiment

Provide groups of students with the leaves, the fasteners, and wax paper. They may use the small dolls or stuffed animals as models. Allow them time to create. Each group should make one hat from each type of leaf.

When finished, students record what each hat looks like, carefully describing the colors and textures of each hat. You may want them to measure the length of the hat and record that as well. After a day, have the students observe the leaf hats, and again record specifically what they see. After several days, observe, and record again.

Wrap It Up/Expected Outcomes

Have students draw conclusions about Tom Thumb's hat, and record their conclusions on the activity sheets.

What will happen: The leaves will quickly lose any rigidity they had. They will become limp, and the color may darken. Then they will dry, and the edges may curl up. As they become older, any fasteners students used may loosen or fall apart. *Why?* Without the constant support from the tree, which is their food source, the leaves cannot maintain their shape, color, and rigidity. They will quickly start to wither. Tom could not have worn a leaf hat for very long!

Tom Thumb #1
Tom Thumb's hat was made out of an oak leaf.

Would an oak leaf really make a good miniature hat? Are there other leaves that would work also? Would the hat wear well? Would it be good quality?

Science Spark **What would happen to a leaf hat over time?**

Make a hypothesis: Make a statement that tells how you think a miniature hat made out of leaves would hold up if worn day after day.

My hypothesis:

In this experiment, you will make some tiny hats out of leaves. You will use a fresh **oak leaf**, and **two other kinds of leaves** that can be folded or bent into a hat shape. List the three types of leaves you have collected:

_____   _____   _____

Bend and fold the leaves you collected to look like hats. You may want to fit the leaf hats onto the heads of a small doll or stuffed animal. You can use pins, staples, or other fasteners to help your leaf hat keep its shape.

Tom Thumb #1

Place the leaf hats on wax paper (or on your dolls' heads) and study them carefully. Describe each hat below. Be specific, telling about the color(s), size, and textures.

Hat #1

Hat #2

Hat #3

Leave the hats, and return the next day to again look at the leaf hats. Describe them.

Hat #1, Day 2

Hat #2, Day 2

Hat #3, Day 2

Describe the hats after three or four days. What is happening to the leaf hats?

Hat #1, Day #___

Hat #2, Day #___

Hat #3, Day #___

Draw conclusions. Could Tom Thumb have worn a leaf hat over time?

Tom Thumb
BACKGROUND INFORMATION

Tom Thumb #2

Science Spark __What happens to batter when it is boiled?__

Science Area/Principle Physical Science, Chemistry, Matter

Additional Materials Needed

Dry pasta (1/4 C at the most or 1/2 lasagna noodle,) a carrot, mixing bowl, wooden spoon, flour sifter, cheesecloth, string, saucepan, plate, or saucer (that fits in the bottom of the saucepan), access to a stove top or a single electric burner, plus the following ingredients:

4 oz. Shredded margarine, Crisco™ or butter	½ C Oatmeal	Rounded tsp baking powder	1½ tsp each-ground cinnamon and allspice	2 eggs, beaten
2 ½ C flour	3 oz. Sugar	8 oz. Chopped raisins	1 tsp light corn syrup	3-4 tbsp buttermilk

The Lesson

Set It Up

Read <u>Tom Thumb</u>. Talk about the pudding that Tom's mother made. What actually happens to food when it is boiled? Do you boil pudding? Have students **make a hypothesis** about what actually happens to food when it is boiled.

Conduct the Experiment

Tell students that the pudding Tom's mother made is not a *pudding* as we know it. It is more like a cake and is a Scottish treat called a *clout* (pronounced 'clout' or 'clootie') after the <u>cloth</u> in which it is boiled. In the experiment today, students will observe what happens to a pudding, pasta, and a carrot when they are boiled.

Place a carrot and the pasta in a pan of boiling water while you prepare the pudding.

Have your students assist you however you feel is helpful in making the clout. It's a great math lesson on measurement! Keep them away from the stove top/electric coil.

In a large bowl, sift the flour, and add the margarine, mixing with a wooden spoon. Add the dry ingredients, and mix. Make a well, add syrup and eggs, and mix well. Add enough milk to make a soft but firm batter.

Remove the carrot and the pasta and set aside.
Dip the cloth in boiling water, shake off excess water, lay flat, and flour it well. Add the mixture to the floured surface. Pull the cloth up to create a rounded batter ball, and tie the top of the cloth with string, leaving enough room for expansion. Place a saucer in the bottom of the saucepan, and stand the dumpling on top. Cover with boiling water, and boil for 2 ½-3 hours. (Refill water as needed so that the clout stays at least 2/3 covered.)

Tom Thumb
BACKGROUND INFORMATION

Tom Thumb #2

Wrap It Up/Expected Outcomes

Assist the students in answering some of the questions on the activity page. *How hot will the water get?* (212°) *Why does it bubble?* (Heated water turns into water vapor, which is a gas. Gas is lighter weight and comes to the surface of the water and is released.)

While the pudding is cooking, have students examine the pasta and carrot, and record what they notice happened to them. The pasta and carrot soak up some of the hot water and are not only a little bigger, but softer. Were they chemical changes or a physical change? (Physical change)

Examine the pudding when it is finished. (It is a chemical change – the ingredients no longer exist in their original form, and something totally new has been produced.)

There are many variations to this clout pudding. Some include: ginger and nutmeg, the zest of lemons, and currants and sultanas. In Scotland this holiday treat is not only a treat for the mouth, but a gift to the pocket book! Sometimes coins are wrapped in greased paper and baked inside the pudding. The cook just needs to let the diners know, so there are no broken teeth!

Tom Thumb #2

TomThumb's mother made a pudding by wrapping batter in cloth and boiling it!

Can you make a pudding by putting it in cloth and boiling it? Is that how pudding is normally made?

Science Spark **What happens to batter when it is boiled?**

Make a hypothesis: Make a statement that tells what you think happens to batter (or other foods) when they are boiled.

My hypothesis:

In this experiment, you will work with your teacher to make some pudding the old fashioned way! You will find out what happens when batter is boiled and what happens to some other foods when they are boiled.

What foods is your class boiling in the experiment? List them below.

Food #1

Food #2

Food #3 *the batter* (List several of the ingredients you see your teacher add to the batter.)

Tom Thumb #2

Watch as your teacher gets some water to boil. How hot will the water get? _____ ° F

Why does it bubble?

Look closely to see what happened when the foods were boiled for a few minutes. Describe each of the foods' appearance after it was boiled. How is it different?

Food #1

Food #2

Food #3

Did all of the foods react to boiling water in the same way?

What do you think happens to food when it is boiled? Write your conclusions.

Tom Thumb
BACKGROUND INFORMATION

Tom Thumb #3

Science Spark   Are you nearsighted?

Science Area/Principle   Health Science, Anatomy

Additional Materials Needed

Snellen eye chart (you can download an eye chart from www.i-see.org or ask a local optometrist for a donation. If you print an eye chart from the Internet, check the calibration line at the bottom. It should be 100 mm. If it is not 100 mm, multiply the length x 2.36. That yields the distance in inches to stand so that the test will be accurate.) A sign, poster board-sized (any ready-made sign, or handmade sign. Unpredictable text is preferred,) a typed letter or series of paragraphs, tape

The Lesson

Set It Up

Read and review details of <u>Tom Thumb</u>. Recall that a nearsighted hawk picked up Tom. What does it mean to be nearsighted? Have students **make a hypothesis** that tells if they think they are nearsighted.

Conduct the Experiment

Divide your students into three groups. Each group will rotate after performing eye tests at each location.

Center **#1**- Students will stand 20 feet from the Snellen eye chart, covering one eye at a time to read with first the right, then left eye. Another child in their group can assist in marking the lowest line that was successfully read aloud. Students will record their results on the activity sheets.

Center **#2**- Students will try to read the letter, holding it at arm's length in front of them. They will look at the item with just the right and then left eye. They will describe how well they could see the item, using words such as *clear, blurry, fuzzy* etc.

Center **#3**- Students will stand in the hall and try to read the sign that you will hang prior to the activity. Have students stand 50 feet from the sign, view it with the right and then the left eye, and record how well they could read it.

Wrap It Up/Expected Outcomes

Ask students to think about how well they saw the items in each task. Do they think they see near things better, far things better, or both equally well? Ask them to draw conclusions and record them on their activity sheets.

Tom Thumb
BACKGROUND INFORMATION

Tom Thumb #3

After students draw their conclusions and record them, share and discuss what it means to be nearsighted or farsighted. Some students may be very concerned if they experienced some blurriness in these activities.

Myopia (nearsightedness) – distant objects are blurred, the condition usually develops in school age children, and it may be hereditary, 30% of people in the U.S. have myopia.

Hyperopia- (farsightedness) –- near objects are blurred, people with hyperopia have trouble concentrating, and may suffer from headaches.

(Astigmatism is a common eye problem in which objects are blurred at all distances.)

Inform students that as they grow, so do their eyes. These vision problems are caused by the eyes' misshape. So, eye problems may get better as they grow, or may appear in the coming years, even when their previous eye exams were fine.

Today's experiment certainly cannot replace a visit to the optometrist. But do try to explain what the numbers mean on the Snellen chart. On the eye chart, the numerator reflects the distance the reader is from the chart. The denominator is the maximum legible viewing distance. So if your sight is 20/30, you are standing the required 20 feet from the chart, and you could legibly read the chart if you were 30 feet away.

Tom Thumb #3

The nearsighted hawk mistook Tom for a toad.

What does it mean to be nearsighted or farsighted? How do your eyes work? What do people mean when they say their sight is 20/20?

Science Spark **Are you nearsighted?**

Make a hypothesis: Make a statement that tells if you think you are nearsighted.

My hypothesis:

In this experiment you will be using your eyes to see how well you see things in order to determine if you are nearsighted or farsighted! You will test both your eyes because no two eyeballs are alike! You will rotate through three centers with your group.

First, your group will take turns looking at a standard eye chart. Measure 20 feet from where the eye chart is posted and place a line of tape on the floor. Take turns. Stand behind the tapeline and look at the chart. Cover one eye and try to read every line on the chart. Then cover the other eye and try to read the chart again. Write down how you did:

Right eye: I was able to read the letters well on the _____ line.

Left eye: I was able to read the letters well on the _____ line.

Tom Thumb #3

At the next center, pick up the letter. Hold it in front of you, at about arm's length. Cover one eye at a time, and alternate looking at the item with your right and left eye. Can you read it? Describe your success below, using specifics like *blurry, fuzzy, clear etc.*

Right eye:

Left eye:

Now, take turns going into the hall. Your teacher has set up a sign that is far away. Look for the tapeline on the floor. Stand behind the tapeline and see if you can read the sign. Describe how well you did. Use specific adjectives to describe how you saw the sign.

Right eye:

Left eye:

Think about what the objects and signs looked like to you. Were you able to clearly see the items or were they blurry and out of focus? Were you able to see just as well with each eye?

Draw conclusions about your eyesight. Write your summary below. Do you think you are nearsighted like the hawk in Tom Thumb?

*This activity does not diagnose your eyes! You should see an optometrist every year for an eye exam.

Hansel and Gretel
OVERVIEW

Story version used: classic retelling by Scott Gustafson

Hansel and Gretel #1

Science Spark What is the difference between a new moon and a full moon?
Science Area/Principle Earth Science, Physical Science, Light Energy
The Lesson Students will hypothesize about the amount of light from the moon that would reflect off pebbles. They will create different 'night boxes,' each with a hole cut to let light in. The holes represent different moon phases.

Hansel and Gretel #2

Science Spark How did Hansel and Gretel know when it was noon?
Science Area/Principle Earth Science, the Sun
The Lesson Students will hypothesize about how Hansel and Gretel could have told time outdoors. They will observe shadows over time to see how a sundial works.

Hansel and Gretel #3

Science Spark What creatures would eat your breadcrumb trail?
Science Area/Principle Life Science, Animals
The Lesson Students will hypothesize about who would eat crumbs left behind. They will then leave a trail of crumbs outside and observe over time what comes to eat them!

Hansel and Gretel #4

Science Spark How can windows be made out of sugar?
Science Area/Principle Physical Science, Chemistry, Matter
The Lesson Students will hypothesize about how to make a glass material from sugar. They will assist the teacher to make a recipe for sugar glass.

Hansel and Gretel #5

Science Spark How well would you be able to identify different smells?
Science Area/Principle Health Science, Human Body, Senses
The Lesson Students will make a hypothesis that explains how well they can smell. They will test their sense of smell by smelling to see which students in their class are members of their 'pack.'

Hansel and Gretel
OVERVIEW

Research Extensions

Hansel and Gretel's father was a woodcutter.
Find out how trees are cut down now compared to how Hansel and Gretel's father would have cut them. What is the salary of a present-day woodcutter?

Math Extensions

Hansel filled his pockets with pebbles.
How many pebbles would it take to fill your pants' pockets? How much would that weigh? How far would that many pebbles stretch if you dropped one every 6 feet?

After leaving the witch's house, they walked for two hours.
How far did they walk if they walked for two hours? How can you figure that out without actually walking for two hours?

Hansel and Gretel
BACKGROUND INFORMATION

Hansel and Gretel #1

Science Spark <u>What is the difference between a new moon and a full moon?</u>

Science Area/Principle Earth Science, Physical Science, Light Energy

Additional Materials Needed

Four shoeboxes, black craft paper, glue, tape, utility knife (like an Exacto™ knife,) four or more light colored 1-2" pebbles, four flashlights

The Lesson

Set It Up

Read <u>Hansel and Gretel</u>. Discuss the different ways that Hansel brainsormed to help the two siblings find their way back home. Which one worked? Would that really work? Why? Have students **make a hypothesis** about how the phase of the moon affects how much light will reflect off objects.

Conduct the Experiment

Students will work in small groups to create a Moon Shadow Box that represents one of the phases of the moon. Divide students into groups and assign them one moon phase. (Provide them with resources to research what their phase looks like.) First, students will cover the inside of the shoebox with black paper. Then they will draw a 2" tall image of their moon phase centered on one short end of the shoebox. The teacher uses the knife to cut out the moon phase, as well as a thin, horizontal slit on the opposite short side. Place pebbles in the boxes. You may have one pebble or actually make a pathway inside the box. Replace the lid.

Students place a flashlight behind the moon phase and tape in place.
Each student takes a turn to look in the slit and observe the light that is reflected off the pebbles. They need to look at the reflected light off the pebbles. They should not look directly at the flashlight light. If it seems too bright, diffuse it by placing wax paper over the flashlight before placing it up to the moon phase cutout.

Wrap It Up/Expected Outcomes

After viewing all the Moon Shadow Boxes, students will complete the table on the activity sheets and record their conclusions.

Remind students that the moon does not produce its own light; the light we see from the moon is actually reflected off the sun. Discuss the results. Students should have observed that the more light that is allowed to enter the box, the more light is reflected to the surrounding walls of the box. Similarly, the more light given off by the actual moon, the easier it would be to find your way home in the dark. So Hansel and Gretel would have had an easier time returning home if the moon had been full.

Talk about some other variables:

⇨ Would the color of the pebbles make a difference in the reflection of light? If time permits, place some darker colored pebbles in the boxes and observe them again. What if the sky was cloudy?

Hansel and Gretel #1

The pebbles shone brightly in the moonlight so that Hansel and Gretel were able to find their way home.

Would white pebbles shine in the moonlight? Would other colors of pebbles reflect light as well? Would it make a difference if the moon were a new moon instead of a full moon?

Science Spark **What is the difference between a new moon and a full moon?**

Make a hypothesis: Make a statement that tells how the moon phase affects the light reflected off pebbles.

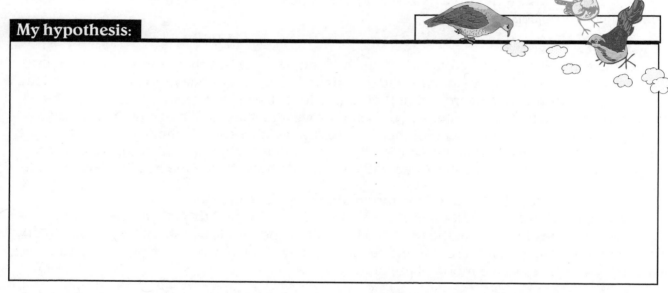

My hypothesis:

In this activity you will see if light really reflects off pebbles and if light from the different phases of the moon matters?

Work with your group to prepare Moon Shadow Boxes! Take a shoebox and cover the inside with black paper. Listen for directions. Research what the moon looks like in one of these phases: full, quarter, half, new. Draw the correct shape on one of the short sides of the shoebox. Make the moon 2" tall. Your teacher will help you cut out the moon shape and a small hole on the opposite side for you to peek into the box.

A flashlight shown into the moon end of the box will serve as your moonlight! (*But remember - it's actually sunlight that is reflected off the moon. The moon does not provide its own light.)

Hansel and Gretel #1

Place a pebble inside your Moon Shadow Box and replace the lid. Turn on the flashlight. Take turns in your group to peek into the box. Is the light reflecting off of the pebble? Do you notice any light from the pebble being bounced to the black paper on the sides of the box? Record in the chart below what you see. Repeat for the other moon phase shadow boxes.

	Circle one				*give details*
Full	Dim	Bright	Brighter	Brightest	
Half	Dim	Bright	Brighter	Brightest	
Quarter	Dim	Bright	Brighter	Brightest	
New	Dim	Bright	Brighter	Brightest	

Take another look if you need to! Reflect on what you have seen.

Write your conclusion about how the phase of the moon affects the light that is reflected.

Hansel and Gretel
BACKGROUND INFORMATION

Hansel and Gretel #2

Science Spark How did Hansel and Gretel know when it was noon?

Science Area/Principle Earth Science, the sun

Additional Materials Needed
Craft sticks, paper plates, clay, masking tape

The Lesson

Set It Up
Read Hansel and Gretel. They were left on their own with some bread for lunch. And they saved the bread until lunch! How did they know when it was time to eat? Have students **make a hypothesis** about how Hansel and Gretel could have known it was noon.

Conduct the Experiment
Students will be going outside at several times to observe the sun in two different activities to see if they can tell time by the sun.

Activity One: Students will mark a spot on the ground outside and view the sun. (*Caution students not to look directly at the sun.*) Students need to find a comparison point for the sun's position. (Is it at the top of a flag pole, to the right of a certain tree, etc.) They will record this position. Students will return to the same marked spot at least three more times during the day. Each visit they will record the time and where they see the sun in relation to the comparison point. Is it now above that point, 10 feet to the left, etc.

Activity Two: Students will make their own sundials. Students use clay to affix a craft stick or pencil vertically in the center of a paper plate. Take plates outside and place them in full sun. Instruct students to mark the first shadow with a pencil line and mark the time of day. Include A.M. or P.M. When you return to make observations for Activity #1, also mark the next shadow and label the time on the sundial.

Wrap It Up/Expected Outcomes
After the observations have been done, have students make conclusions about whether or not Hansel and Gretel would be able to tell when it was noon by reading the sun's position in the sky. Data should show from both activities that the sun is highest in the sky around noon. Some variations occur depending on where you live. For Activity One, the sun will seem to move higher and away from the comparison point. The direction depends on if they were facing **N** or **S**. The sundial pencil lines will have moved as well, extending in a clockwise direction.

Discuss what factors could change these results. What if it was cloudy or rainy?

Hansel and Gretel #2

They ate their bread when noon arrived.

How did Hansel and Gretel know it was noon without a watch? If you were in the forest, how could you tell time?

Science Spark How did Hansel and Gretel know when it was noon?

Make a hypothesis: Make a statement that tells how you would tell time outdoors.

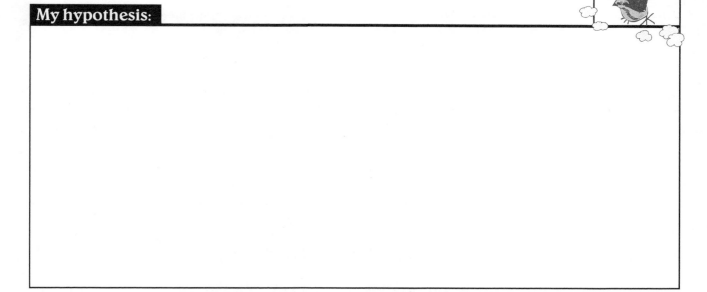

My hypothesis:

Have you heard *the sun rises in the east and sets in the west?* It's true. Although, it isn't the sun moving. The Earth is rotating. As the Earth rotates on its axis, the eastern part of the country sees the sunrise first. At the end of the day, the Earth has rotated so far that we can't see the sun anymore. The position of the sun in the sky has helped people tell time for thousands of years. Today, you will do two different activities to see if you can tell time from the sun.

1. Go outside and find the sun. (Do Not stare directly at the sun.) Mark a spot on the ground with tape. You will keep careful records each time you observe the sun so that you can see where the sun will be at noon. Then you will know what Hansel and Gretel may have been looking for. <u>Record the time you observe the sun in the sky</u>. Also, write notes that remind you of the position of the sun in the sky. Is it just above the roof top, touching the top of a flag pole?) Return three more times, and repeat the observation from the same spot.

Hansel and Gretel #2

Observation Time # 1	Notes:
Time # 2	Notes:
Time # 3	Notes:
Time # 4	Notes:

2. Make a sundial. Place a pencil or craft stick in the center of a paper plate. Stand the stick up vertically by putting it in a small amount of clay or putty.

Take the paper plate sundial outside when you go to observe the sun for Activity #1. Place the sundial on the ground where it will get full sun.

With a pencil, mark the place where a shadow is created when the sun hits the stick. Label the time next to the pencil line. When you go outside to make observations for Activity #1, look at your sundial. Mark the shadow with a pencil line again, and do so at least four times at even intervals, recording the time each visit.

Could you tell what time of day it was by looking at the sun? Could Hansel and Gretel have known when it was time to eat their bread? Write your conclusions below.

Hansel and Gretel
BACKGROUND INFORMATION

Hansel and Gretel #3

Science Spark __What creatures would eat your breadcrumb trail?__

Science Area/Principle Life Science, Animals

Additional Materials Needed

Bread slices, cardboard sheets or box lids (lids from copy paper boxes work well,) 1-2 bags of sand, ruler, signs for the *track box* (to ask peers not to walk on the sand)

The Lesson

Set It Up

Read <u>Hansel and Gretel</u>. The trail of pebbles worked, but the trail of breadcrumbs did not. Why not? The birds ate Hansel's breadcrumbs and kept the children from finding their way home. In this activity the students will try to find out what creatures would eat breadcrumbs left on their school grounds by making a *track box*. Have students **make a hypothesis** about what would eat the crumbs.

Conduct the Experiment

As a class, take the cardboard or box lids outside. (You may want to have the sand outside in the 'breadcrumb location' ahead of time, since transporting the sand can be cumbersome and heavy.) Spread out the cardboard sheets. If you are using lids, lay them against each other to create a square sandbox shape. Pour sand on the cardboard or in the lids so that there is a layer of several inches of sand. Take the ruler and use an edge to smooth the sand to a flat, even surface. If permitted, let some of the sand blend down into the surrounding grassy area. You may want to bend the lips of the box lids down.

Have students in small groups take their slices of bread and break them into bite-sized pieces. Scatter the pieces in a path in front, across, and beyond the *track box*.

Students should observe the sand space to see what creatures come to eat the crumbs. If your classroom has a window, students can monitor the box periodically during the day through the window. If not, have students go outside one more time during the day and record what creatures are seen in the area, if any. Are there any footprints in the sand?

The next day, return as a class to the site of the *track box*, and observe what footprint tracks have been left in the box. Have students draw the tracks in the spaces provided on the activity sheets. Ask students to identify the animals that made the tracks.

Wrap It Up/Expected Outcomes

Ask students to record their conclusions, based on the data they collected from the *track box*. Discuss the tracks that were found. Are there any surprises? Are the expected animal tracks represented inside the sand box? (You can expect to see bird and squirrel prints and possibly a raccoon if you live in an area close to woods. We've found rooster and deer prints at our school as well!) How would this experiment change if you only observed during the school day and did not leave the trap overnight? Why?

Hansel and Gretel #3

Hansel dropped pieces of bread so that they could find their way home, but the birds ate the bread, so they had to remain in the forest.
If you made a breadcrumb trail, would the birds eat the crumbs?
Who else might eat the crumbs?

 **What creatures would eat your breadcrumb trail?**

Make a hypothesis: Make a statement that tells who you think would eat breadcrumbs left outside.

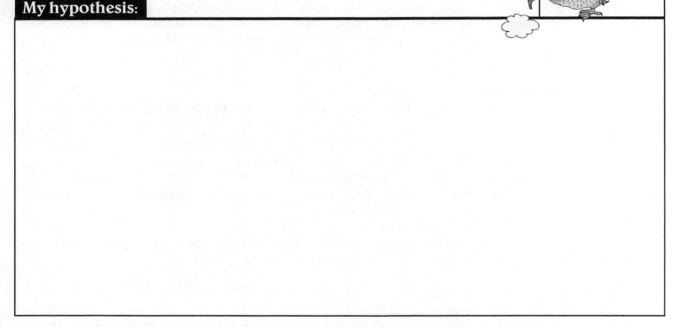

My hypothesis:

Today you will be placing a '*track box*' outside to see which animals that like to eat bread are living around your school grounds. If any animals come to eat the crumbs, they will hopefully leave tracks in the sandy *track box* for you to find!

Go outside and help your teacher set up the *track box*. Your teacher will let you know where you can help spread the sand. Take a ruler and run it across the top of the sand so the top surface is smooth. Make sure no one walks in the sand! *You may want to put up some signs for your peers, letting them know that this is a science project, and ask them not to disturb the site.

Now, break up the bread into small, bite-sized pieces. Together with your classmates, scatter the crumbs in a path that runs down the center of the sand *track box*.

Hansel and Gretel #3

*Optional: If your classroom has a window and the trap is visible outside it, take turns watching for a few minutes each hour to see if you can catch any wildlife coming to eat the crumbs. If not, go outside in pairs. Record below who/what is seen coming to munch:

Wait for 24 hours. (Many animals may only come out to eat at night while you're at home!) Go outside and see if the crumbs are gone. If they are, are there any tracks in the sand? Below, draw pictures of the tracks you see in the sand.

To what animals do you think the tracks belong? If you think you know, write the animal's name inside the box next to the sketch of the track. Did the animals you expected come to eat the bread?

Write your conclusions about the creatures that live on your school grounds.

Hansel and Gretel
BACKGROUND INFORMATION

Hansel and Gretel #4

⟨Science Spark⟩ <u>How can windows be made out of sugar?</u>

Science Area/Principle Physical Science, Chemistry, Matter

Additional Materials Needed

Aluminum pie tins or aluminum foil and shoebox lids, sugar, water, light corn syrup, spray cooking oil, heavy saucepan with lid, access to a stove top, spoon,
Optional items: candy thermometer, food coloring, food flavorings

The Lesson

Set It Up

Read <u>Hansel and Gretel</u> and discuss Gretel's favorite part of the witch's house - the sugar windows! Ask students if they think you can really make windows or glass from sugar. Students will **make a hypothesis** about what is needed to make sugar glass.

Ask students to share any information they have about materials from which 'real' glass is made (sand mostly, and a little lime and sodium oxide.)

Tell students that you can make a type of glass out of sugar. (Sometimes this 'sugared glass' is used in stunts by actors because it shatters like glass but won't hurt them!)

Conduct the Experiment

The students will be assisting and <u>observing</u> as you prepare the material for sugar glass. Temperatures will be very hot, and the heat source and the sugar/water mixture could easily burn someone. The following recipe is enough for one pie tin. Double as needed.

Boil 1 cup water and then add 2 cups of sugar and ¾ cup of light corn syrup. Return to a boil. Cover the pan for 2 minutes. Remove the cover and continue boiling for another 10-12 minutes. You should have a good, rolling boil. (If you have a candy thermometer, the mix should reach 310°.) Remove mix from heat. Quickly add food coloring and any food flavoring you want. Pour into the prepared (greased) pie tin and let it cool for 90 minutes.

Wrap It Up/Expected Outcomes

You may want to try this at home before trying to make it during the lesson. You don't need a candy thermometer, but it will help you know if you have reached 'hard crack' and can remove the mix from the heat.

After 90 minutes, the sugar glass will be solid and should slide off the greased tin. You should be able to see light through it. How much light depends on any color you tinted the mixture and how thick the mix was in the pan. Be careful, it's breakable!

Discuss the results with the students. Does it look as they expected? Have them record their conclusions on the activity page.

If you flavored the sugar glass, have a taste like Gretel did!

Hansel and Gretel #4

Gretel enjoyed the sugar windows and ate more and more of them.

Could windows be made out of sugar? Would you be able to see through them? What happens if it rains?

Science Spark How can windows be made out of sugar?

Make a hypothesis: Make a statement that tells how you think you could make sugar windows.

My hypothesis:

Have you ever made and eaten rock candy? Rock candy is made when sugar collects on a wooden stick as it crystallizes from oversaturated sugar water. How can we have sugar harden flat and smooth like a pane of glass?

First, you will be working to make molds for the windows. Carefully take a sheet of aluminum foil. Press and crease it on top of a cardboard shoebox top. Press carefully. You want the foil nice and flat with four sides sticking up over the lips of the box top. This is the mold for your sugar glass window and the sides need to keep the solution from leaking out. (Be careful not to poke a hole in the foil with your fingers; it rips easily.)

Take a paper towel with some cooking oil on it or a can of cooking spray and grease the bottom of the mold. This will make it easy to remove the window once it is cured.

Watch and help your teacher if needed, as the sugar glass mixture is made. List the ingredients your teacher is using. Circle the ingredient that in used in the biggest amount.

Hansel and Gretel #4

After the mix boils for over 10 minutes, it is poured into the mold you prepared. Did your teacher add any flavoring to the mixture right before it was poured? If so, what flavor?

After 90 minutes, the sugar glass is ready! After your teacher slides it out of the mold and holds it up to the light, observe the sugar glass. Describe the glass below.

Write your conclusions about how to make glass out of sugar.

Why do you think it would be more difficult to make a larger pane?

Hansel and Gretel
BACKGROUND INFORMATION

Hansel and Gretel #5

Science Spark How well would you be able to identify different smells?

Science Area/Principle Physical Science, Chemistry, Matter

Additional Materials Needed

One different scent per small group, (scents should be easily recognizable from each other; for example, a few different perfumes, one men's cologne, a spice such as cinnamon, a food flavoring such as vanilla, one empty film canister per student (or you may soak in the scent one piece of cardboard per student, and place the cardboard in a zippered bag to avoid evaporation.)

The Lesson

Set It Up

Read Hansel and Gretel. The witch always knew where the children were because of her keen sense of smell, which was lucky since she didn't see well! Pose the question to the students - could you sniff out members of your family? Ask students to **make a hypothesis** about how well they think they could find other members of their group by relying on their sense of smell.

Conduct the Experiment

Beforehand decide how many small groups you will have. Prepare sets of film canisters for each group. For example, you may have 25 students. Prepare 5 sets of 5 canisters, each set having a unique scent. To prepare the canisters, pour a small amount of the scented liquid (or bit of the spice) into the film canister and close the lids tightly. Scramble the canisters.

During the lesson, pass out a film canister to each student. Read the directions on the activity sheet together. Instruct them about how they are to smell their own scent only <u>once</u>, then travel the room sniffing other people! Describe how you want them to move about the room. They should always walk. Specify a path, if you want an organized movement, or let them freely roam about the room.

When they think they have found a member of their '*pack*' they should stay together. When they think they have the whole *pack* they should stop and stand together. Even if all groups are not formed, you may want to have a time limit and announce the end of the sniff session.

Wrap It Up/Expected Outcomes

When the sniff session is over, have students record their reactions to the level of difficulty in finding your *pack* using only your sense of smell. Some students may find it difficult to recall their own scent after smelling so many other scents in the room.

Students should record their conclusions to the hypothesis on the activity sheets.

Hansel and Gretel #5

The witch had a very keen sense of smell, like a wild animal.
How well do wild animals smell? Do animals have a better sense of smell than humans?

Science Spark How well would you be able to identify different smells?

Make a hypothesis: Make a statement that tells how well you think you could find members of your group by only using your sense of smell.

My hypothesis:

You are a member of a certain group out in the wild, a pack! Your task is to get all the members of your group together. But, you don't know who the other members of your group are yet!

You will have to use your <u>sense of smell</u> in order to find the other members of your group. Follow the directions below to find the members of your pack!

1. You will be given a container that contains a scent. You will have a few seconds to smell the scent of your *pack*.

2. When your teacher tells you to, open the container and take a sniff. Try to remember the smell. (Most scents contain a kind of alcohol, which evaporates quickly, so close the container quickly and tightly.)

3. You will carry your scent around, but <u>you will not smell it yourself again</u>. When your teacher gives the word, you will move about the room. When you come to another classmate, smell each other! (Each other's containers.) Is s/he a member of your *pack*? (Make sure you get your original container back.)

4. When you think you have found a member of your *pack*, stick together, and travel as a *pack*. Keep moving around the room until you have sniffed all your classmates!

5. Listen for when your teacher ends the sniff session.

Hansel and Gretel #5

Reflect on the activity. How hard was it to keep the memory of your scent in your mind once you started smelling lots of other scents? Do you think you could pick out a smell in the wild and follow it like many animals can?

Write your conclusions about how well you were able to use your sense of smell to identify members of your pack.

*It's easier to find things by sight. How easy would it be to find members of your pack using your sense of hearing **only**?*

The Three Little Pigs
OVERVIEW

Story version used: classic retelling by Scott Gustafson

The Three Little Pigs #1

Science Spark Could wind (or a wolf's breath!) blow a house down?
Science Area/Principle Earth Science, Weather
The Lesson Students will hypothesize about the strength of wind. They will make models of straw, twig, and brick houses and test their construction with wind from a hair dryer.

The Three Little Pigs #2

Science Spark How much cooler is the air in the shade than the air in the sun?
Science Area/Principle Earth Science, Light Energy
The Lesson Students will hypothesize about how the sun changes the temperature of the air. After placing thermometers in various places on school grounds, students will collect data about air temperature and form conclusions.

 ## Research Extensions

The wolf wanted to eat the pigs.
What do wolves prefer to eat? Find out if they normally eat pigs or if other animals are more to their liking.

The three pigs' mother looked out for them.
Do sow mothers care for their young? If so, for how long?

 ## Math Extensions

The wolf landed in boiling water.
How hot is boiling water? What is the difference between boiling water and freezing water? Find out the difference in both Fahrenheit and Celsius.

The Three Little Pigs
BACKGROUND INFORMATION

The Three Little Pigs #1

Science Spark <u>Could wind blow a house down?</u>

Science Area/Principle Earth Science, Weather

Additional Materials Needed

Cardboard (for the bases of each group's house), straw (wheat or pine straw) small twigs or drinking straws, thread, Legos™ or other connecting toy blocks, hair dryer, tape, rulers

The Lesson

Set It Up

Read the <u>Three Little Pigs</u>. Review how each of the pigs chose to make their houses out of different materials. Why do you think they chose those materials? Would a strong wind really be able to blow over a whole piggy house? Have the students **make a hypothesis** about what would happen if a strong, concentrated wind hit a house of straw, twigs, and bricks. The students will prepare these types of houses to withstand a wind test.

Conduct the Experiment

Break the students into three groups, and assign each group one of the types of houses that the pigs built: straw, twig, and brick. Pass out the materials to each group and allow them time to pick up and study the materials and discuss with their group how to use it to make a house. The houses should be square or rectangular, about 4-6" in each direction. Remind the groups that no glue, tape, or other fasteners can be used except for thread. Allow students enough time to make their houses. When complete, they need to be firmly affixed to a piece of cardboard.

Each house will have the same test. Decide where the hair dryer will be mounted/held. Have the students work together to measure and mark distances of 24", 18", and 12" from the hairdryer. Then, test each one. First, place the house 24" away from the 'wind.' Have students observe what happens and record on the activity sheets. If the house withstands the first blast, move it closer to the 'wind' source and again test, observe, and record. If the house still stands, move it to within a foot of the 'wind' and repeat. Conduct the same tests for each of the other two houses, stopping after each distance to allow the students to record their observations.

Wrap It Up/Expected Outcomes

After all houses have been tested, ask students to make their conclusions about wind damage. Do they think any wolf could really blow down a house? It is most likely that the straw house will be ruined with the first, and certainly the second blast of wind. The twig house might make it up to 12" before it is destroyed, and the brick house should be unharmed at all distances. (Be sure the houses are firmly attached to the cardboard bases so that the whole house doesn't just slide off the board in tact.)

The Three Little Pigs #1

The wolf huffs and puffs and blows down the straw and twig houses.

Science Spark **Could wind (acting as the wolf's breath) blow a house down?**

Make a hypothesis: Make a statement that tells what you think would happen if a wind current was concentrated on a straw, twig, and brick house.

My hypothesis:

In this activity, you will play the part of the pigs, and the part of the wolf will be played by…a hair dryer! You will work in groups to construct a model of a straw house, a twig house, or a brick house. You will use the materials provided by your teacher: straw for the first pig's house, and thin sticks or drinking straws for the second pig's house. You may not use glue, tape or other fasteners. You may use thread. You may use connecting blocks, such as Legos™.

1. Work with your partners to make a small model house that is between 4-6" tall and about as wide. Take your time as you begin this activity to talk with your group about how best to design and construct your model house. Take time to manipulate the materials to see how you can weave them or in some other way attach them to each other.
2. Place and anchor your model house to a piece of cardboard.

When your models are complete, it is time to test them out!

Your teacher will hold the hair dryer so that the airflow travels across the top of a flat surface, like a table or desk. Measure 24", 18", and 12" from the front of the hair dryer, and place a labeled tapeline at each distance.

Place the **straw house** on the 24" line. Tape the cardboard base of the house to the table. Turn on the hair dryer and look closely. Record what happens at the 24" line. If the house survives, move it to the 18" line, test, observe, and record. Repeat at 12" if possible.

The Three Little Pigs #1

STRAW HOUSE

24"	18"	12"

Now test the **twig house** in the same way. Watch closely, and record what happens.

TWIG HOUSE

24"	18"	12"

Now, test the **brick house** in the same way. Watch closely, and record what you see.

BRICK HOUSE

24"	18"	12"

Draw conclusions about how well the wolf could have blown the houses down, based on your experiment.

What is the likelihood that wind or strong air currents could blow down a house?

The Three Little Pigs
BACKGROUND INFORMATION

The Three Little Pigs #2

Science Spark **How much cooler is the air in the shade than the air in the sun?**

Science Area/Principle Earth Science, Light Energy

Additional Materials Needed

Two thermometers per small group, two wooden craft sticks or tongue depressors per small group, watches (optional)

The Lesson

Set It Up

Read The <u>Three Little Pigs</u>. When it was lunchtime, the hard-working pig ate his lunch in the shade. Ask students why they think the pig may have chosen to eat in the shade instead of in the sun. Students may share answers like, '*The pig wanted to lean up against a tree*' and hopefully will suppose, '*It is not as hot in the shade.*' Inform the students that today they will be conducting an experiment. Students should **make a hypothesis** to see if the air is cooler in the shade than it is in the sun.

Conduct the Experiment

Using the activity page, read the directions with the students. Before going outside, have each small group write their group name boldly on the craft sticks that will serve as their marking sticks. Take the small groups outside, along with their marking sticks and thermometers.

Find an area on school grounds where students will be able to mark a spot and leave a thermometer in the shade and in the sun. (If the area is well traveled by other classes, you may want to prepare some signs to mark the experiment or alert fellow teachers asking their assistance in keeping the experiment site undisturbed.) Each small group of students should deposit their stick and thermometer in a suitable spot, wait a few minutes for the thermometer to register a more accurate temperature, and record the time and temperature on their activity sheet.

Return to the classroom. Students should return to their areas three more times, each time recording the time of day and temperatures of each spot. (As the sun moves, the shade may shift. Let students know that it is acceptable that they move their mark and thermometer a little bit in order to keep it in the shade.)

Wrap It Up/Expected Outcomes

When the students have completed all readings, have them bring in the markers and thermometers after their last visit. Discuss aloud, asking groups to share their data and any pattern they see in their results. Do they think the pig made a wise choice?

The readings should show that it is indeed cooler in the shade. (The difference in temperature between the two depends on the weather on the day of the experiment and the season.)

The Three Little Pigs #2

The second pig lays in the shade to eat his lunch. Why would the pig make a point to eat his lunch in the shade?

Science Spark **How much cooler is the air in the shade than the air in the sun?**

Make a hypothesis: Make a statement that tells what you think the difference in temperature is between being in the sun and being in the shade.

My hypothesis:

In this activity, you will be collecting data about air temperature to see if there is a difference in temperature between a sunny place and the shade. If there is a difference, how much of a difference is there?

You will be working in a group to collect and record air temperature data.
1. Decide on a name for your group.
2. Write your group's name clearly on each of two craft sticks.

Along with your teacher, go outside and find a sunny spot and a shady spot. Bring along two thermometers and your marking sticks. Place one of your group's markers and a thermometer in the sun, and one thermometer and marking stick in the shade.

Record the time that you placed the thermometers outside: _____

Record the temperature in both places: sun: _____ shade: _____

The Three Little Pigs #2

You will leave the thermometers, and return to the marked sites several times. Wait between 30 minutes and an hour between each recording.

Air temperature check #1: time: _____ temperature: *sun* _____ *shade* _____

Air temperature check #2: time: _____ temperature: *sun* _____ *shade* _____

Air temperature check #3: time: _____ temperature: *sun* _____ *shade* _____

What has happened to the air temperature as the day warmed up? Think about the data that you have recorded and come to a conclusion.

Is it cooler in the shade?

Write down your conclusion about the temperature difference between a shady spot and a sunny spot.

The Twelve Dancing Princesses
OVERVIEW

Story version used: classic The Brothers Grimm

The Twelve Dancing Princesses #1

Science Spark What wears down a pair of shoes?

Science Area/Principle Physical Science, Physics

The Lesson Students will make a hypothesis about why their shoe soles wear out. They will then score and scratch their sample 'shoes' on different materials in order to observe the effects of friction.

The Twelve Dancing Princesses #2

Science Spark How does adding weight affect the effort needed to move an object?

Science Area/Principle Physical Science, Physics

The Lesson Just as the soldier noticed it was harder to row three people across the lake, the students will feel the extra energy that is needed in an experiment that pulls classmates across the floor on a cardboard sled. Students will hypothesize about how added weight changes the energy needed to move an object.

The Twelve Dancing Princesses #3

Science Spark Why do some branches make a snapping sound when they are broken?

Science Area/Principle Earth Science, Botany

The Lesson Students will make a hypothesis about why some tree branches make an audible snapping noise when broken, since others do not. Students will then snap and break off different types of food 'sticks' in order to help them draw a conclusion about the rigidity and moisture of branches.

 ## Research Extensions

The soldier saw trees whose branches had leaves of silver, gold, and diamonds.
Where are these natural resources really found?

 ## Math Extensions

The princes had three nights to figure out where the princesses dance. But they were all unable to discover the answer.
How many shoes were ruined in that time?

The princesses danced until 3 A.M.
If they started dancing at midnight, how many hours of dancing is that? How many minutes?

The Twelve Dancing Princesses
BACKGROUND INFORMATION

The Twelve Dancing Princesses #1

 **Science Spark** __What wears down a pair of shoes?__

Science Area/Principle Physical Science, Physics

Additional Materials Needed

'Shoe,' test surfaces, wood, staples, ballet slipper (optional)

For each small group of students, a test 'shoe' cut from heavy cardboard, compressed leather (if available,) foam board, or other similar material; two different surfaces on which to scrape the shoe. The test surfaces should vary. Some should be smooth (so that very little wear occurs) while other surfaces should be designed to leave a lasting impression on the shoe. These test surfaces may be different types of sandpaper, metal grating, carpet samples all stapled to woodblocks, rocks adhered to wood or contained in a box, etc. *Be sure that the surfaces will not injure a child if their hand slipped from the shoe and scraped on the test surface.

The Lesson
Set It Up

Read or remind students about the dancing princesses. Discuss how they wore out their shoes every night! Look at a ballet slipper and discuss its sole as well as the soles of the students' shoes. Why do some shoes wear out quickly or unevenly? Have the students make a hypothesis about why shoe soles experience wear. Have them record the hypothesis on their papers.

Discuss three important vocabulary words. (These terms are part of *Tribology,* which is a science that includes the study of friction, lubrication, erosion, and wear.)

Score – to score something, in this sense, means to leave directional grooves or striations

Scratch – to scratch means to displace or remove material from an object

Wear – damage to a solid object and the progressive loss of material because of motion between the object and a surface it comes in contact with.

Conduct the Experiment

Divide the students into small groups of 2-4 students each. Students will take turns rubbing the shoe against each surface, in each of the two directions. For scoring, they will move the shoe only forward and backward. For scratching, they can move the shoe in a circle, or back and forth.

The Twelve Dancing Princesses
BACKGROUND INFORMATION

The Twelve Dancing Princesses #1

After each rubbing the students need to examine the shoe for change and record what they see in the chart on their activity page. *You may want to keep a *control* of their shoe for comparison. You may also direct the students to touch the bottom of the shoe right after they rub it. Is it warmer than before?

Wrap It Up/Expected Outcomes
Outcomes will vary depending on the shoe material and the test surface materials that are used. If the students 'score' correctly, they should observe grooves or stripes in the shoe. When they 'scratch' they should notice that the actual material of the shoe has been torn, shifted, or removed.

The shoe will wear out because of <u>friction</u>. Friction is the resistance to push or pull and produces heat, of course - but also causes wear.

There are three kinds of friction: *sliding, rolling,* and *fluid.* The students' experiment involved sliding: moving two surfaces against each other.

Students should record their conclusions about the wear and tear of shoe soles. They may want to reexamine their own shoe soles. Is it evident that one area on the sole has been rubbing on surfaces more than others? Is there a certain way the student walks or runs that is causing wear?

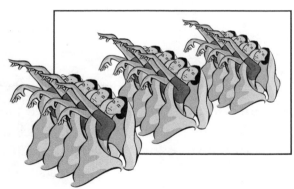

The Twelve Dancing Princesses #1

The daughters wore their shoes to pieces every night.

How much dancing would it take to wear out a pair of shoes? Could you wear down shoes in one day?

Science Spark **What wears down a pair of shoes?**

Make a hypothesis: Make a statement that explains how you think shoe soles get worn.

My hypothesis:

Look down at the soles on your shoes. Is there any evidence of wear and tear on them? Look at your neighbor's shoe. Whose shoes look newer? Does it have anything to do with the style of shoe, the size of the shoe, or the activities of the wearer? In this activity you will experiment to see if you can discover why shoes show wear.

Your teacher will give you a 'shoe' sole. You will *score* and *scratch* the shoe on different surfaces so that you can observe what happens. If you are working with a partner, take turns to press the shoe sole on the test surface following the directions for scoring and scratching.

Score – to imprint directional grooves or striations. Move the shoe forward and backward.

Scratch – to displace or remove material. Move the shoe in a circular pattern.

The Twelve Dancing Princesses #1

You will have two test surfaces. On each surface, *score* and *scratch* the shoe. Record what you observe on the shoe sole after each rubbing.

Test Surface #1	Score	
Test Surface #1	Scratch	
Test Surface #2	Score	
Test Surface #2	Scratch	

Does your shoe look worn? Which surface and which motion do you think caused the most wear on the shoe sole?

Draw conclusions. What causes your shoes to wear out? Use any science vocabulary you feel explains the process.

The Twelve Dancing Princesses
BACKGROUND INFORMATION

The Twelve Dancing Princesses #2

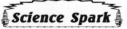 **How does added weight affect the effort needed to move an object?**

Science Area/Principle Physical Science, Physics

Additional Materials Needed

A cardboard 'sled' to act as the boat, rope, masking and duct tape (optional)

 The Lesson

Set It Up

The sled should be big enough for 2 students to sit on. Cut two slits in one of the end flaps. Thread rope through and tie it in a loop. Be sure the slits are several inches from any edge in case they rip. You may want to fortify the holes/slits with heavy duct tape in order to prevent ripping. Use masking tape to mark the *start* line and *finish* line 10 feet away.

Clear an area in the classroom that is several times wider than the piece of cardboard. Place the cardboard on the floor. (This experiment will vary depending on whether your room is carpeted or not. It will be easiest if you have tile floor. To make it easier you may move into a hallway depending on the age and strength of your students.) You could substitute a wagon for the cardboard sled if you have one.

Review the trips across the water in *The Twelve Dancing Princesses*. When the soldier invisibly joined the boat, the prince found it much harder to row. Tell the students that they are going to experience what the prince did in order to draw conclusions about how much harder one has to work when more weight is added to a load. Of course, there isn't a lake available, so the experiment will have to be on dry land.

Conduct the Experiment

Allow different students to take turns, either being on the 'boat' or being the 'rower.' The 'rower' in this experiment is actually pulling the cardboard sled. Students should try to slowly move the sled 10 feet to the finish line. After pulling one student, reset the sled, and add a child. Again, the rower should try to move the sled 10 feet.

Not all your students may be able to play the part of the rower. Have those that do describe aloud how they felt as they tried to move the sled. All students should record the observed outcomes on their papers.

Wrap It Up/Expected Outcomes

Whether you use a wagon or the cardboard sled, the students who pull should have voiced a noticeable difference in the effort needed to move it. There is <u>friction</u> involved. Ask the students to think about the difference between rowing in water and pulling on land. Which has less friction? From a physics standpoint, the amount of force needed to move freight is proportional to the amount of force pushing one surface against the other. If the sled is twice as heavy, then the force needed to move it will need to be two times greater, since there is twice as much force pushing the sled to the floor.

The Twelve Dancing Princesses #2

The boat was harder to row when the soldier secretly joined it.

How much difference can one man make? Why was it harder to row the boat?

Science Spark **How does added weight affect the effort needed to move an object?**

Make a hypothesis: Make a statement that explains how adding weight changes effort needed to move something.

My hypothesis:

Are you good at Tug-of-War? Could you pull a classmate 10 feet across the floor? What about two or three classmates?

In this activity you will do an exercise (and get some exercise) in order to find out!

Your teacher has a cardboard sled. This is like the boat in the story, and you may play the part of the prince, the princess, or the soldier. As your teacher directs you, take turns trying to move the sled 10 feet across the classroom floor.

With the sled lined up at the START line, pull the sled with one passenger. Pull until you reach the FINISH line. Describe below how it felt to move the sled.

The Twelve Dancing Princesses #2

With the sled once again lined up at the START line, try to pull the sled again the 10 feet to the FINISH line. How did it feel this time? Record in the space below your reactions to how much effort you had to use.

Did you notice a difference between the first pull and the second? How *much* harder was it to move two people?

Do you think it would be easier or more difficult to move freight on a boat across the water? Explain your reasoning?

Draw conclusions. How does adding weight (increasing the load) change the effort and energy needed to move it?

The Twelve Dancing Princesses
BACKGROUND INFORMATION

The Twelve Dancing Princesses #3

Science Spark __Why do some branches make a snapping sound when they are broken?__

Science Area/Principle Earth Science, Botany

Additional Materials Needed

Two - three tree branches (gathered carefully to prevent injuring a tree) one 'green' and the other dry/dead, stiff food 'sticks' such as celery, large pretzels, bread; softer food sticks such as green onion or scallions, bananas, etc., paper plates or paper towels

The Lesson

Set It Up

Discuss the portion of The Twelve Dancing Princesses where the soldier breaks off branches to take with him. The snapping noise almost gives him away. Show the students two different tree branches. Attempt to 'snap' them. The 'green' branch should bend but not break or snap. The dried branch will snap. Have the students make and record a hypothesis about why they think some branches make a noise while others do not.

Conduct the Experiment

Give small groups of students some different food 'sticks.' Instruct the students to snap the sticks in half, paying close attention to what happens and what the inside of the stick looks like. You may choose to give different groups varying sets of food. Students need to record all their observations in the appropriate chart. They should begin to form some opinions about the material in the sticks that do snap and those that do not.

Wrap It Up/Expected Outcomes

Begin a discussion on the students' findings, having them share. Record on the board or large chart whether each food stick snapped and what the students noticed about the inside.

The food that was similar to a living, green branch (green onions, cheese, etc.) should not have snapped, but should have only bent. The dry food sticks (pretzels, breadsticks) should have snapped. Branches (and food) that are still moist will not snap. The moisture keeps the plant material more pliable, flexible. Internal parts of the plant cell called vacuoles are filled with water and minerals and actually supply pressure against the cell wall. Living plants and trees are *turgid*- swollen with water. Dry food or branches no longer have any moisture to assist in flexibility and support, so they snap easily.

The Twelve Dancing Princesses #3

The branches made a loud snap each time the soldier broke off a piece.

The loud snap almost gave the invisible soldier away. Why did the branch snap aloud?

Science Spark Why do some branches make a snapping sound when they are broken?

Make a hypothesis: Make a statement that explains why you think branches make a snapping sound you can hear.

My hypothesis:

In the story, the soldier is taking back some mementos from his secret trip with the princesses. But the snapping of the branches almost foiled his plan to remain in secret. Have you ever walked in the yard and had branches snap beneath your feet? Why do some sticks snap audibly while others do not? Today you will manipulate some different sticks to see if you can discover a clue to solve the mystery.

Your teacher will give you several different kinds of food 'sticks.' You will need to break each stick in half. Look carefully as you snap the stick. What happened? Examine the inside of the stick. How does it look? As you snap each new food stick, look at the inside. Record your observations. Write the name of the food under the appropriate heading, and describe what you notice about the stick and its inside.

The Twelve Dancing Princesses #3

Foods that **snap and break**	Foods that **bend and do not break**

What are some similarities between the sticks that snapped in half and made a noise?

What are some similarities between the sticks that did not snap?

Draw conclusions. Write your final thoughts about what makes a branch snap.

Cinderella
OVERVIEW

Story version used: classic retelling by Scott Gustafson

Cinderella #1

Science Spark What is left over after a fire?
Science Area/Principle Physical Science, Chemical Change
The Lesson Students will make a hypothesis about what happens when things burn and whether or not burning materials always produces cinders or ashes. They will then observe their teacher burn various items in order to draw conclusions.

Cinderella #2

Science Spark How does soap work?
Science Area/Principle Physical Science, Chemistry
The Lesson Students will hypothesize about how soap is able to clean. Students will use several different kinds of soap to see which is most effective in cleaning spots.

Cinderella #3

Science Spark How does a trumpet's size determine its sound?
Science Area/Principle Physical Science, Sound Energy
The Lesson Students will make a hypothesis about which aspects of a trumpet determine its sound. They will experiment with different-sized tubes of different materials in order to draw a conclusion about size and sound.

Research Extensions

The sisters drew the laces of their corsets tight so that they would appear thinner. Many women did this centuries ago, and it made them pass out!
What happens to your lungs when they are squeezed tightly? How does it cause you to pass out or faint?
What were *fainting couches*? Who used them and when?

Math Extensions

How many legs were on the creatures that helped Cinderella?
How many legs did they have after they were transformed?

Cinderella
BACKGROUND INFORMATION

Cinderella #1

Science Spark **What is left over after a fire?**

Science Area/Principle Physical Science, Chemical Change

Additional Materials Needed

Matches or propane lighter (for the teacher ONLY), a variety of materials to burn, such as paper, wooden craft stick, wool yarn, cotton scraps, plastic spoon (with extreme caution - plastics can release dangerous gases. Do this outside, or burn it ahead of time, and bring the result out later,) peanut, olive oil, aluminum foil, safety goggles
DO NOT burn any item that has been painted, as many paints are toxic when burned.

The Lesson

Set It Up

Discuss how Cinderella got her nickname. Review that she was covered in cinders from the fire she had to tend. Ask the students: *What are cinders? Is there a difference between cinders and ashes? When something burns, does it always create cinders or ashes?* Have the students make and record a hypothesis about what they think happens when something burns. *What is left behind?*

Conduct the Experiment

In a WELL-VENTILATED area, lay out each of the objects to be burned on their own piece of aluminum foil. One item at a time, ask students to guess what will happen as it is burned. Ask them to pay close attention - to not only wait for the outcome, but to watch the flame's color and size as it is burning. They will need to record all their observations on their activity sheets. Be sure the students stay a safe distance from the burning. Repeat for each item. Leave each item on the aluminum foil for inspection at the end.

Wrap It Up/Expected Outcomes

Purposely, the items chosen here will not all produce cinders or ashes. Fire is a chemical reaction produced by oxygen and a heated fuel of some kind. Different fuels will produce a different burn and a different end product. Wood, for example, needs to reach about 300° Fahrenheit. The wood will decompose and the cellulose will burn. Gases are released (smoke) and the unburnable materials will be left as ashes or char. From your experiment, you can expect to see the following:

Paper - grayish ashes	Plastic spoon - melt and distort, turn black
Wood stick - grayish and black ashes	Peanut - will burn (may take a few tries)
Wool - shiny black ashes	Olive oil - oil will cause the flame to go higher-
Cotton - dull black ashes	(Use a skewer that is lit, and place it in the oil)

Have the students think about why materials burn and what they leave behind. Have them draw and record their conclusion about fire's byproducts on their activity sheets.

Cinderella #1

Cinderella gets cinders all over herself from being so near the fire.

What are cinders? What are ashes? Does fire always leave cinders?

Science Spark **What is left over after a fire?**

Make a hypothesis: Make a statement that explains what material or substance is left over after a fire has burned something.

My hypothesis:

In this activity, you will examine what materials are left behind after something burns.

Fire is a <u>chemical reaction</u>. The materials that are left over after burning don't just *look* different - they *are* different. The heat has changed the material.

Cinderella #1

You will watch as your teacher burns a variety of materials. Fill in the name of each item as it is burned. Watch CAREFULLY. Record what you see during and after each burn. Write your observations in the table below.

Paper
Wood stick
Cotton
Plastic spoon
Peanut

Examine what the items look like now that they have been exposed to fire. Why did they not all leave ashes behind? Draw conclusions about what was left behind after each fire. What kinds of substances did you see left over? Record your conclusions.

Cinderella
BACKGROUND INFORMATION

Cinderella #2

Science Spark How does soap work?

Science Area/Principle Physical Science, Chemistry

Additional Materials Needed

Dirty 'clothes' with visible dirt, various fabric scraps with stains from dirt and food, bar soap, liquid hand soap, laundry soap powder, access to a sink or small tubs of water, vegetable oil (optional)

The Lesson

Set It Up

Review that Cinderella had to scrub floors. *What did she most likely use to scrub the floors clean? What makes soap clean a surface? How does it work? Are some soaps better than others? Do the amount of bubbles a soap produces have any correlation to how well that soap works?*

Tell students that today they will need to clean their dirty clothes! They will be testing soap to see if it cleans and how well. Each group will have small amounts of the three types of soap listed above. They will test these soaps on their dirty 'clothes.'

Conduct the Experiment

Have students work together in small groups. (As you set up the fabric scraps, it is best to use all of the same kind of fabric so the fabric weave type does not alter how well it is cleaned of dirt.) Give each group three scraps, all with the same stain. For example, Group A will test clean jelly stains, Group B will test mud, etc.

Students will need to record what their stain looks like at first, and measure the diameter of the stain. They need to record the information in the chart on their activity pages. Then have the students wet the scrap in a tub of water or in a sink. Have them rub the stain with one of the soaps and watch what happens as the stain and soap react with each other. Again, they record their observations. Repeat this until all three pieces have been cleaned.

Wrap It Up/Expected Outcomes

Gather the students around a glass of water. Drop in some vegetable oil. What happens? The oil will not mix with the water. Drop in a dab of liquid soap and watch what happens. Explain to the students that soap is an *emulsifier.* It allows one liquid to spread into another. Soap has two jobs: it breaks *surface tension* and it sticks to *dirt, grime ,and bacteria.* Soap is made up of acids and bases. Fatty acids (such as oils) bind to dirt. They are called *hydrophobic.* The *hydrophilic* (salts and hydrocarbon elements) allow the *hydrophobic* molecules to grab and actually encapsulate the dirt so that it can be washed away. As long as soap has the ability to do these things, it will clean. The amount of suds and bubbles does not mean a better cleaning soap, nor does a fragrance. Each group should share aloud their results, as they all have different 'dirt' to clean. Have students draw conclusions about how soap works, and record them on their activity pages.

Cinderella #2

Cinderella is forced to scrub the floors.

What would she have used to scrub the floors? Do some soaps work better than others?

◢Science Spark◣ How does soap work?

Make a hypothesis: Write a statement that explains how you think soap works to clean a surface.

My hypothesis:

Remember poor Cinderella having to clean and scrub? Scrubbing floors requires some elbow grease, but it also requires soap. How does soap work to clean away dirt? Do you think that some soaps work better than others? Do you need a lot of bubbles to get clean?

You will need to clean your dirty clothes today! You and partners will get fabric scraps with a stain on them. Your job will be to test three different kinds of soap as you attempt to clean your 'clothes.'

After your teacher puts you in groups and gives you your dirty laundry, record the type of stain you will be washing: _____

Cinderella #2

Now, use a ruler and measure the <u>diameter</u> of the stain. Record the diameter and your observations of the color and texture of the stain in the chart, under 'BEFORE.'

Soap #1:	Soap #2:	Soap #3:
BEFORE: d =	BEFORE: d =	BEFORE: d =
AFTER: d =	AFTER: d =	AFTER: d =

Did your soaps get your laundry clean? Share with your classmates how well your soap worked on your stain. Draw conclusions about the effectiveness of soap. How do you think the soap is able to work? Write your conclusions below.

Cinderella
BACKGROUND INFORMATION

Cinderella #3

⫴ Science Spark ⫴ How does a trumpet's size determine its sound?

Science Area/Principle Physical Science, Sound Energy

Additional Materials Needed

Cardboard tubes of different sizes or card stock, Optional materials: a trumpet or cornet, other musical wind instruments

The Lesson

Set It Up

Remind students that in the story of <u>Cinderella</u>, trumpets were used to announce the arrival of the prince. Trumpets are still used today for fanfare and as 'announcers' due to their crisp, clear and enjoyable sound. Why does the trumpet make that sound? What determines the sound instruments make? Ask students to make a hypothesis about what determines the sound a musical instrument will make.

Conduct the Experiment

You can use cardboard toilet paper, paper towel, and wrapping paper tubes, or make your own out of cardstock of various lengths. Each student should have their own tubes since they will be placing their mouths on them. Teach students to 'buzz' their lips. Allow them to practice. (If they hum or sing into the tubes, they will not produce the proper sounds.)

Each student will buzz into one end of each tube in turn. They need to listen carefully for the sound they produce. They can repeat as often as they need until they hear the differences in pitch. After making the sounds, students need to indicate on their activity sheets which tube made the highest, medium, and lowest pitch.

*For an added experiment, selected students could demonstrate blowing over the top of plastic water/soda bottles. Have bottles that are almost full (it is difficult to get a sound from a full bottle), half full, and empty. Ask students to listen to the differences in pitch.

Wrap It Up/Expected Outcomes

On the activity page, have students record a conclusion to the question *What determines the sound an instrument makes?* Students should have noticed that the longer the tubing , the deeper the sound that is produced. (Or, the more air space in the water bottle - the deeper the sound.)

Think about instruments in the orchestra. The piccolo/flute is short and produces a very high-pitched sound. The trumpet is bigger with more twisting tubes. The tuba is even larger and has long tubing. It has a deep sound. The tube length affects the pitch. (Instrument material affects the *timbre* or quality of sound. If the tubes in this experiment were plastic or metal, the pitch would still vary but the *timbre* would be different.) The more rapidly an item vibrates, the higher the frequency. Frequency determines pitch. (High frequency=high pitch=short wave length.)

Cinderella #3

Trumpets heralded the arrival of the prince.

Why are trumpets used for fanfare? Why do they sound the way they do?

Science Spark **How does a trumpet's size affect its sound?**

Make a hypothesis: Write a statement that explains how you think the size of a musical instrument affects the sounds we hear.

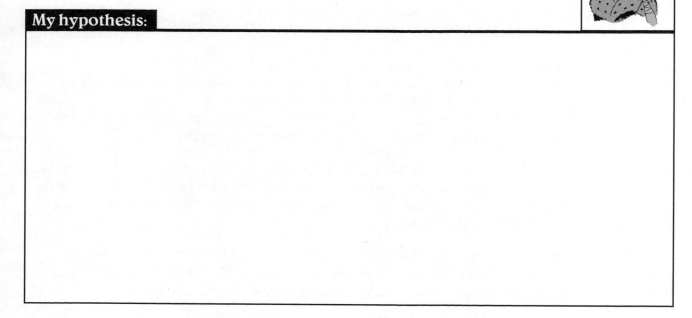

My hypothesis:

Trumpets were used to announce that royalty were coming. They are still used today to announce, or herald, important events. The trumpets of centuries ago looked a lot different than today's, but they made their sounds the same way. What determines the way a musical instrument will sound?

Today you will experiment with different tubes in order to make a judgment about why instruments sound the way they do.

First, listen as your teacher shows you how to '**buzz**' your lips. You will make a sound just like you were playing a brass instrument with tubing. Practice. Be sure not to sing or hum. You have to buzz and vibrate your lips. It tickles!

Cinderella #3

You will need to buzz into one end of each of three tubes. Listen carefully to the difference in sound. You may need to buzz on each tube a few times. In the chart below, circle the word that <u>best</u> describes the **pitch** (highness and lowness of sound) you heard from each tube.

Short tube (toilet paper roll)	High pitch	Medium pitch	Low pitch
Medium tube (paper towel roll)	High pitch	Medium pitch	Low pitch
Long tube (wrapping paper roll)	High pitch	Medium pitch	Low pitch

Think about the results and what you heard. What do you think makes an instrument have a high or low pitch?

Write your conclusion.

The Giant with the Three Golden Hairs
OVERVIEW

Story version used: classic by the Brothers Grimm

The Giant with the Three Golden Hairs #1

Science Spark Why didn't the heavy wood sink?

Science Area/Principle Physical Science, Physics

The Lesson Students will make a hypothesis about why a box of heavy wood did not sink in the water. They will then create and attempt to float different clay 'boats' in order to draw conclusions about why some objects can float while others of the same weight may sink.

The Giant with the Three Golden Hairs #2

Science Spark What determines hair color?

Science Area/Principle Life Science, Chemistry

The Lesson Students will hypothesize about what makes hair come in different colors. They will then examine different hair samples under a microscope, viewing the cortex of the hair, sketching what they see, and drawing a conclusion about how hair color is determined.

 ## Research Extensions

In what countries did kings and queens live in the 15th, 16th and 17th centuries? What countries still have active ruling kings and queens?

 ## Math Extensions

If the lake is one mile across, how many miles might the ferryman row in an average day?

The Giant with the Three Golden Hairs
BACKGROUND INFORMATION

The Giant with the Three Golden Hair#1

 **Science Spark** Why didn't the heavy wood sink?

Science Area/Principle Physical Science, Sound Energy

Additional Materials Needed
Modeling clay (not Play-doh™), sink, bowls, or tubs of water, pennies

The Lesson

Set It Up
Remind the students that although the box was made of wood and contained a weight in it (the boy!) it did not sink. How is that possible? How do some things that are heavy have the ability to float? Tell the students they will be experimenting with different designs to create a 'boat' that will float and hopefully a boat that will float with weight in it. Have them record a hypothesis about why heavy objects are able to float.

Conduct the Experiment
Briefly discuss water displacement. When an object is placed on the surface of the water, it presses down on the water at the same time as the water presses up on it. Ask students to keep this in mind as they prepare to make their boats.

Give each student a ball of modeling clay to create a boat. As they finish a boat, have them bring it to a tub of water to see if it floats. They need to watch and record what happens. Have students try several different times, recording each time what happened and how they changed their design.

When the boat *does* float, start adding pennies to it. Keep adding pennies until the boat sinks. Count the pennies, and record the number of pennies on the activity page.

Wrap It Up/Expected Outcomes
Have students draw conclusions about what makes a boat float, and record them on their activity pages. Discuss aloud which design types seemed to work better than others. Whose boat held the most pennies?

In addition to pressure between the water and the boat, the key to floating is that the object has to *displace* an amount of water that is *the same as* its own weight.

The Giant with the Three Golden Hairs #1

The box with the boy in it did not sink.

Why did a wooden box not sink? Why do some things sink while others float?

Science Spark **How are heavy objects able to float?**

Make a hypothesis: Write a statement that explains how you think a heavy boat is able to float.

My hypothesis:

Think about the boy set to float in a wooden box. How was he able to float when wood is so heavy? Today you will be making a boat of your own design to see if you can make it float. You will also weigh down your boat, and see if it can still float.

Your teacher will give you a piece of clay. Mold the clay into a *boat*. When you are finished with your first design, take it to the water tub, and test it out! Be sure to watch closely so that you can record your observations. If your boat floats, add pennies until it sinks.

The Giant with the Three Golden Hairs #1

Record the number of pennies your boat was able to carry.

Boat #	Brief description of the design	Did it float?	# of pennies
1			

Try again with a new design. Test it, and watch carefully. Fill out the chart below.

Boat #	Brief description of the design	Did it float?	# of pennies
2			

Try again with a new design. Test it, and watch carefully. Fill out the chart below.

Boat #	Brief description of the design	Did it float?	# of pennies
3			

Were you a master boat builder? Was it difficult to get your boat to float? What do you think is important in order to have a boat successfully float?

Draw conclusions about what makes a boat float, and record them.

The Giant with the Three Golden Hairs
BACKGROUND INFORMATION

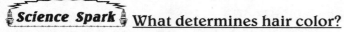

The Giant with the Three Golden Hair#2

Science Spark <u>What determines hair color?</u>

Science Area/Principle Life Science, Chemistry

Additional Materials Needed:
Microscope, glass slides, water dropper, hair samples

The Lesson

Set It Up

The grandmother in the tale pulled hair from the giant's head. The hair was golden. Why was it golden? What makes a person's hair the color it is? Yes, your parents matter, but it more specifically has to do with the hair itself. Ask the students to think about what makes hair the color it is and record their hypothesis on their activity pages.

Conduct the Experiment

You can use hair samples that you have prepared previously, or you can ask if anyone wants to pull their own hair! You will undoubtedly have some volunteers. Be sure that your hair samples are a range of colors - blonde, red, brunette, and black, and are *wet mounted*. Some science supply companies do sell pre-made slides of hair, even dog and cat hair! Check with your local science lab to see if there are any slides you may borrow.

The students will be looking in the microscope at each of four slides and then drawing what they see on their papers. If you have the supply, set up four microscopes, and allow the students to travel to each one, pausing to draw what they see while others take a look. If you only have access to one or two, your experiment will take more time.

Be sure the students draw as detailed a picture as they can. To see the inner (cortex) of the hair, you will probably need to pre-focus the medium lens. Under low power, you may only see the outer cuticle of the hair. Students need to view the cortex of the hair shaft.

Wrap It Up/Expected Outcomes

The outer part of the hair is called the cuticle. It looks like overlapping scales or bark on a tree. Looking deeper, you should be able to view the cortex. This inner shaft of the hair contains proteins. Within those proteins are granules of a pigment called *melanin*. The melanin is what determines hair color. There are two types of melanin: *Eumelanin* and *phaeomelanin*. The eumelanin is responsible for brunette and black hair, and the phaeomelanin is evident in red and blonde hair shades. Many times the hair has a mixture of these two. Eumelanin granules look like little pearls. Phaeomelanin appears more like ovals or footballs with a less defined boundary. Looking at the drawings the students made, they should see that the presence of more round (eumelanin) that made dark hair color, while the presence of more oval-shaped granules created red or blonde hair.

The Giant with the Three Golden Hairs #2

The grandmother pulled out one of the giant's golden hairs.

Why is your hair the color it is? What determines hair color in people (and animals!?)

Science Spark **What determines hair color?**

Make a hypothesis: Write a statement that explains how you think a person's hair gets the color it has.

My hypothesis:

The giant had golden hair. Do you have golden hair? Most people in the world actually have black hair. Why do people have different hair color? There is actually a chemical reason for it! Today you will examine hair under a microscope in order to see for yourself why hair comes in different colors.

The Giant with the Three Golden Hairs #2

Your teacher has set up microscopes. Carry this page and a pencil as you rotate to the different microscopes. View the hair. Your teacher has already focused the microscope so that you can see inside the hair sample. DO NOT adjust the microscope without permission.

Each time you see the hair magnified, study it. Draw it below. Be precise.

Hair Sample #1 - hair color: _____	**Hair Sample #2:** _____
Hair Sample #3: _____	**Hair Sample #4:** _____

Look at your drawings. Can you determine what makes a difference in a person's hair color? State your conclusions.

The Golden Goose
OVERVIEW

Story version used: classic by the Brothers Grimm

The Golden Goose #1

Science Spark How fast does milk spoil?
Science Area/Principle Physical Science, Microbiology
The Lesson Students will make a hypothesis about what causes milk to spoil. They will then set up an experiment of different types of milk left out to spoil, keeping careful records in order to develop a conclusion.

The Golden Goose #2

Science Spark How do feathers keep a bird warm?
Science Area/Principle Life Science, Ecology
The Lesson Students will make a hypothesis about how feathers are effective in keeping birds and ducks warm. They will experiment with two different conditions in order to draw a conclusion about feathers' efficacy in keeping birds warm.

The Golden Goose #3

Science Spark How does glue work?
Science Area/Principle Physical Science, Polymers
The Lesson Students will think about glue and hypothesize about how glue adheres things together. They will test glue to see how quickly it dries on different surfaces.

The Golden Goose #4

Science Spark How do feathers keep a bird dry?
Science Area/Principle Life Science, Ecology
The Lesson Students will make a hypothesis about how feathers are effective in keeping birds dry. They will experiment with two different materials in order to draw a conclusion about how feathers keep birds dry.

Research Extensions

The princess drinks from a brook and then a river.
What is the difference between brooks, rivers, streams, or creeks?

The clever son cut down trees.
Find out the closest location where trees are cut for paper, furniture, or building supplies.
Is there a way to tell the age of a tree without cutting it down?

Math Extensions

The king sees the princess standing in a courtyard. What shape are courtyards usually? Does your school have a courtyard? What is its area?

The Golden Goose
BACKGROUND INFORMATION

The Golden Goose #1

Science Spark How fast does milk spoil?

Science Area/Principle Life Science, Microbiology

Additional Materials Needed

12 small half-pint cartons of milk - three each of whole, two percent, and skim; a heat lamp or consistently sunny spot, 12 clear, see-through plastic or glass containers, plastic wrap, tape, and pens

The Lesson

Set It Up

Engage the students in a discussion. The son carried a jug of milk into the forest. After having left the milk out for hours before he had lunch, would the milk have spoiled? What makes milk spoil? How fast does it happen? Does the type of milk make a difference? Have the students make a hypothesis about what the biggest cause of milk spoilage is, and have them record it on their papers.

Conduct the Experiment

You should be able to easily get the milk cartons from your school cafeteria. You will conduct an experiment with three kinds of milk (to see if the fat content matters) in four different situations (to see if location makes a difference and to see if added bacteria makes a difference.)

In small groups, have the students pour each type of milk into a clear container. As they do this they need to label the container with the type of milk that is inside. They need to cover the top with plastic wrap, pull taut, and tape so that no more air can get in. You will direct them where to store the milk. You will have four different locations:

1. Put one set of containers in a refrigerator.
2. Put a second set in a room-temperature spot, away from direct sunlight.
3. Put a third set in a similar spot as #2; however, have a child drink a little bit of milk from each cup before sealing the top. This will add more bacteria to the cup for the purpose of seeing if the additional bacteria will speed spoilage.
4. Set the last group of containers under a heat lamp or in a sunny spot.

Students should describe the look of the milk on this first day of the experiment. Revisit the milk briefly each day until you notice some spoilage (see explanation.) Students should complete their activity pages and draw a conclusion about how fast milk spoils and why. They need to record their conclusion.

The Golden Goose
BACKGROUND INFORMATION

The Golden Goose #1

Wrap It Up/Expected Outcomes

Milk spoils because of the presence of bacteria. Pasteurization kills a lot of bacteria, but not all. Milk should be kept at 40° F or below. Even so, after a week past the 'sell by' date, refrigerated milk will begin to spoil.

You can tell milk is spoiled by either smelling it for a sour smell (gases given off by the bacteria) or by looking for **separation.** Having students smell spoiled milk is not recommended, so use the separation method. Look for a line between a watery layer and a thicker layer of the milk. If the milk that was NOT opened or touched to a mouth prior to the experiment, the milk in the hot spot will spoil fastest. Heat speeds bacterial growth.

The milk that someone drank from will also spoil faster than the milk that was untouched or the milk that was kept refrigerated. The addition of more and varied bacteria from a human mouth will speed spoilage.

There will most likely not be a noticeable difference in spoilage between the whole, 2%, and skim milk varieties. Although bacteria like fat as a food, the rate at which the milk spoils due to just the fat content will not vary much.

The Golden Goose #1

The clever son carries a jug of milk into the forest.

Why does milk go bad? Does it matter what kind of milk it is?

Science Spark How fast does milk spoil?

Make a hypothesis: Write a statement that explains what you think is the most important factor that causes milk to spoil.

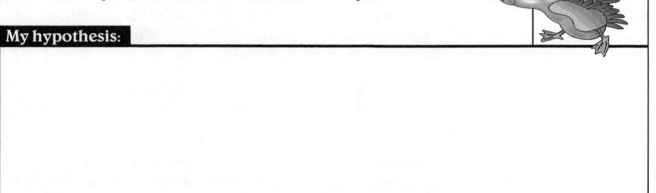

My hypothesis:

If you took milk into the forest and waited a few hours before you drank it, would it still be all right to drink? Or will it have spoiled? What causes milk to spoil?

Today you will be setting up an experiment to see if you can determine how fast milk spoils. You will need to wait several days before you find the answer.

You will work in small groups. Follow the directions your teacher gives you. You will either place milk *in a refrigerator, *in the room, or *in a warm, well-lit spot.

You will be given 3 clear containers and 3 different varieties of milk. For each one:

* Pour the milk one at a time into a clear container.
* Cover the top with plastic wrap, and tape the wrap to the container so that it is airtight.
* Label the container: whole, 2%, or skim
* You may want to make a mark on the container at the highest point of the liquid inside.

Your teacher *may* ask one of you to take a sip from the cups before you seal them, but only <u>one</u> group will be asked to do this. Everyone else should pour the milk, and seal it without touching or sipping the milk.

The Golden Goose #1

Describe below what the milk looks like. Is the milk a uniform color?

In the refrigerator: Day #1   Spoiled! Day #_____

Whole		
2%		
Skim		

Room temperature: Day #1   Spoiled! Day #_____

Whole		
2%		
Skim		

Room temp/sipped: Day #1   Spoiled! Day #_____

Whole		
2%		
Skim		

Warm, bright spot: Day #1   Spoiled! Day #_____

Whole		
2%		
Skim		

The Golden Goose #1

Examine the results. Think about which milk samples spoiled first. What made them go bad before the others did? Were there any samples that never spoiled before the experiment was finished?

Draw conclusions about how fast milk spoils and why, and write them below.

The Golden Goose
BACKGROUND INFORMATION

The Golden Goose #2

Science Spark — How do feathers keep a bird warm?

Science Area/Principle Life Science, Ecology

Additional Materials Needed

For each pair of students 3 zipper closure bags (sandwich size,) water, and ice

The Lesson

Set It Up

Discuss the goose in the story. Birds do not have fur or hair, but instead have feathers. How do these feathers work to keep the bird warm? Some birds live in the arctic, and some spend most of their time on the water, which can be cold! Have the students make a hypothesis about how they think birds are able to keep warm. Ask them to be as specific as possible, and record their hypothesis on their activity page.

Conduct the Experiment

Each pair of students will be given 3 bags. They need to fill one bag half full with water, and add a cup of ice cubes. The second bag should be blown full of air. Students can close most of the top, and then blow in the small opening, closing the bag quickly to retain the air. The last bag will be empty.

Students will take turns. Their hands will play the part of a bird body. Have one student extend both hands, palms up. Their partner will place the empty bag on one hand, the bag of air on the other. They will then place the ice water bag on top of one hand, waiting two minutes. After that time, they will place the bag on the other hand. (It does not matter which hand goes first, as long as both hands have a turn.) The student then needs to record their tactile observations on their paper.

Partners should then switch.

Wrap It Up/Expected Outcomes

When students have finished, they both need to think about their experiment and form a conclusion about how birds are able to stay warm.

Share some information with the students. All birds have two main kinds of feathers: down feathers and contour feathers. The *contour* feathers are interlocking feathers that fit close to the body and aid in waterproofing and airflow over the bird. The inner *down* feathers are soft. They trap air and keep the bird warm. In the experiment students should have noticed that the hand that held the ice bag over the air bag did not get as cold as the flattened, empty bag.

The Golden Goose #2

The goose had golden feathers.

Many birds spend time in cold air currents and water.

Science Spark **How do feathers keep a bird warm?**

Make a hypothesis: Write a statement that explains how you think feathers keep birds warm. Be specific.

My hypothesis:

How do penguins stay warm? How does the goose in the story stay warm while swimming in cold water? Today you and a partner will experiment with two different conditions to see if you can discover just how birds are able to stay warm.

You and your partner will get three zipper-topped bags. Prepare the three bags:
1. Fill one bag half way with water. Add one cup of ice cubes, and seal the bag.
2. Zip the next back almost all the way, leaving a small opening at one end. Blow air into the bag, and quickly seal it the rest of the way.
3. Leave the third bag empty.

Choose who will go first. This person should stand with their hands in front of them, palms facing up. The partner should place the bag of air on one palm and the empty bag on the other. Then the partner should place the bag of ice on top of one palm. Wait two minutes.

If you are holding the bags, what are you feeling? Can you feel the ice water?

The Golden Goose #2

After two minutes, the partner should place the ice bag on top of the other hand. Again, wait two minutes.

Repeat the experiment so that the other person can experience the ice bag.

Record below what you felt when you held the bags. Put an "**X**" in the box that you think most closely resembles what birds have to keep them warm.

Bag of Air	Empty Bag

Think about your experiment results. What keeps a bird warm? Write your conclusion.

The Golden Goose
BACKGROUND INFORMATION

The Golden Goose #3

Science Spark How does glue work?

Science Area/Principle Physical Science, Chemistry

Additional Materials Needed

White school glue, wax paper, copier paper, construction paper

The Lesson

Set It Up

Discuss how in the story all the people got stuck together. *Could people's hands really get stuck together? Is glue that strong? How many kinds of glue are there? (list them!) How does glue work?* Ask students to make and record a hypothesis stating what it is about glue that makes it *adhere* two things together.

Conduct the Experiment

Students will be gluing several items together. Students should cut 4" squares from the three different types of paper provided. Using the white glue, students need to drizzle the glue on a square piece of paper. <u>The amount of glue used should be the same</u> for each square pair, otherwise the experiment will be altered. They should glue A. wax paper, B. copier paper, and C. construction paper. Place papers flat on a table or desktop.

At 10-minute intervals students should check their papers by gently pulling one corner up. They should not pull the entire paper top off. Students need to 'test' each square, and record what they see and feel. *Has the glue consistency changed? Do the papers separate a lot, or just little?* Repeat this 4 times, after which time at least one of the sets of papers should be dry. Which seems to be drying first, or not at all?

Wrap It Up/Expected Outcomes

The papers the students have glued are all paper, but they have different textures and a different amount of small fissures in their surface. The paper with the most cracks and fissures should be the first to be glued/dry. Because there are more crevices for the glue to seep into, it will adhere first. The copier paper (or similarly -notebook paper) should glue second. Wax paper is smooth with few places for glue to seep, so it will be the last to dry, if it ever does dry. The wax also provides a moisture protection barrier discouraging evaporation (see below.)

White glue works through "solvent evaporation." This means as the water in white glue evaporates, the adherent is left. (This type of glue uses poly vinyl-acetate latex.) So in this experiment, as the water evaporated, the glue began to stick. Also, the more porous the surface, the better the seepage was, so the glue worked strongly.

Superglues are different and actually need water in order for them to activate, which is why they adhere skin to skin so well!

For an extension, have students list 'natural' glues. Some are *tree sap, egg yolks, flour and water paste.)*

The Golden Goose #3

Seven people were stuck to each other, running after the boy and the golden goose.

Can glue really stick people together? What is it about glue that makes it stick?

Science Spark How does glue work?

Make a hypothesis: Write a statement that explains why glue works to *adhere* things together.

My hypothesis:

That was strong glue that stuck those seven people together! What kind of material could stick people's hands together? Today you will experiment with safe, white school glue to see if you can discover something about what makes glue work.

Your teacher will provide you with different kinds of paper. You need to cut two 4" squares of each type of paper: A. wax, B. copier, and C. construction.

Place one of each type of paper in front of you. Drizzle some white glue on each square. Do your best to give each square <u>the same amount of glue</u>. Place a square of the same type of paper atop each glued square. Leave them flat on your desktop.

The Golden Goose #3

After ten minutes, <u>gently</u> and slowly pull up one corner of each of the paper squares. DO NOT pull the top all the way off. Just check to see if the glue is drying. What does it look like? Does it feel stiff? Record your observations below.

Time:	A. wax	B. copier	C. construction
Describe what you see and feel…			
Is it dry yet?	Yes/No	Yes/No	Yes/No

Repeat three times, each time 10 minutes apart.

Time:	A. wax	B. copier	C. construction
Describe what you see and feel…			
Is it dry yet?	Yes/No	Yes/No	Yes/No

Time:	A. wax	B. copier	C. construction
Describe what you see and feel…			
Is it dry yet?	Yes/No	Yes/No	Yes/No

Time:	A. wax	B. copier	C. construction
Describe what you see and feel…			
Is it dry yet?	Yes/No	Yes/No	Yes/No

The Golden Goose #3

After the last check, look at all your data. Which paper is glued? Which was dry first? What do you think caused that paper to dry before the others? Come to a conclusion about what makes glue work. Record it below.

For FUN! List all the kinds of glue you can think of.

Natural	Manmade

The Golden Goose
BACKGROUND INFORMATION

The Golden Goose #4

Science Spark How do feathers keep a bird dry?

Science Area/Principle Life Science, Ecology

Additional Materials Needed
Construction paper, wax paper, water sprayers/squirt bottles, sink or tubs, or go outside to test the feathers (optional)

The Lesson

Set It Up
Recall the goose in the story. Birds do not have fur or hair, but instead have feathers. How do these feathers work to keep the bird dry? Even birds that do not spend a lot of time on the water, as a goose might, have the ability to withstand water and rain. Ask the students to make a hypothesis that states how a bird is able to stay dry.

Conduct the Experiment
Students will need two squares of each type of paper. Six-inch squares are an appropriate size. Students will be weaving with the paper. You may pre cut the paper strips and weaving 'frame' depending on the age of the students. Have them weave both the wax paper pieces and then the construction paper. Strips of paper should be pushed tightly against each other so that very little space can be seen between strips.

Tell students that these represent feathers. Now they are ready to test the feathers.

In pairs, students will take turns as one person holds the 'feather' level with the ground. The other person should place one hand a few inches below the feather. With their other hand they will spray some 'rain' over the feather. Does any water filter to the hand below. Repeat with the other feather. Repeat again so the other partner may try.

Wrap It Up/Expected Outcomes
The hand below the construction paper feather probably got quite wet. The hand below the wax paper feather should have stayed drier. (The weave must be tightly done.)

Contour feathers, the outer feathers of birds, are stiff and have barbs that allow them to fit tightly with one another for a barrier. This assists in directing the wind over the bird for improved aerodynamics! Birds have preening glands. They use their beaks to spread oils and fats across their contour feathers. This oil acts as a repellant and keeps them waterproof.
The wax paper has a coating. Therefore, the wax paper woven feather allowed less water to fall below. The construction paper became water logged quickly and let water trickle below, most likely ruining the feather in the process.

Students, realizing that the wax paper was better at keeping their hands dry, should examine the differences in papers in order to come to a conclusion about how birds are waterproof.

The Golden Goose #4

The goose had golden feathers.

Many birds spend time in water, yet don't get wet!

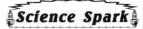 **How do feathers keep a bird dry?**

Make a hypothesis: Write a statement that explains how bird feathers keep them dry. Be specific.

My hypothesis:

Birds spend a lot of time in the water or getting rained on. But they don't get soaked like we would. We don't have feathers! What is it about their feathers that allow birds to stay dry? Today you will experiment with two kinds of 'feathers' to see if you can discover what it is about feathers that keeps birds dry.

You will get two sets of papers: construction paper and wax paper. You will need to <u>weave</u> the paper (under over, under over, etc.) Try to keep the strips of paper close to each other so that there are no gaps in the woven 'feather.'

With a partner, get a spray bottle of water, and stand where your teacher directs you to stand. Decide who is going first. Follow these directions for each person's turn:
1. If you are the <u>bird</u>, hold a *feather* level to the floor a few inches above your partner's flattened hand.
2. If you are the <u>rain</u>, place your hand a few inches below the *feather.* Use the squirt bottle to *rain* on the feather. Spray it several times.
3. Repeat, using the other *feather.*
4. Trade places so each person gets to be the <u>bird</u> and the <u>rain.</u>

The Golden Goose #4

Record your observations below:

What happened when it rained on the construction paper 'feather?'	What happened when it rained on the wax paper 'feather?'

What is it about the feather that kept your hand dry? Think about the experiment and draw conclusions about how birds stay waterproof. Record your conclusion below.

Works Cited

Busch-Vishniac, Ilene J. "Sound." <u>World Book Online Reference Center</u>. 2005. World Book Inc. <http://www.worldbookonline.com/wb/Article?id=ar520640>

Church, Jok R. "Glass Recipe." 12 Feb 2001. <u>Beakman and Jax</u>. 25 Aug 2004 <www.bonus.com/beakman>.

"Cloutie Dumpling." 2004. <u>The Great British Kitchen</u>. The Great British Kitchen. 20 Aug 2004 <www.greatbritishkitchen.co.uk>.

"Content Standards K-4, Science as Inquiry." 2004. National Science Education Standards. 25 October 2004 <www.books.nap.edu>

Elert, Glenn. "Volume of a Human Stomach." 2000. <u>The Physics Factbook</u>. 9 Aug 2004 <www.hypertextbook.com>.

"Feather Anatomy." <u>Microsoft Encarta 98 Encyclopedia.</u> 1998

Gray, John. "The World of Hair." <u>Proctor and Gamble Hair Care Research Center.</u> (2003) 30 May 2005 <www.pg.com>.

Gustafson, Scott. <u>Classic Fairy Tales</u>. Seymour: Greenwich Workshop, 2003.

Harris, Tom. "How Fire Works." <u>How Stuff Works.</u> 2005. 16 April 2005 <http://howstuffoworks.com/fire1.htm

Haury, David L. "Teaching Science Through Inquiry." <u>ERIC</u> ED 359048 (1993). 10 July 2004 <www.ericfacility.net/databases/ERIC_Digests>.

"How does a Heavy Boat Float?" <u>Nautical Know How Inc.</u> (2000) 30 April 2005 <u>www.boatsafe.com</u>

Hultgren, John. "Glue, How Does it Work?" <u>Trivia Collection.</u> 2005. 29 April 2005 <http://john.hultgren.org/trivia/glue.html>

Marzano, Robert J. , Debra J. Pickering, and Jane E. Pollock. <u>Classroom Instruction that Works</u>. Alexandria: ASCD, 2001.

<u>Microsoft Encarta</u>. CD_ROM. 98 ed. 1997.

Morel, Eve , and Roberta Carter. <u>Grimm's Fairy Tales</u>. New York: Grosset and Dunlap, 1962.

"Position Statement." 2004. <u>NSTA</u>. National Science Teachers Association. 7 June 2004 <www.nsta.org>.

Rillero, Peter. "Doing Science with your Children." <u>ERIC</u> ED 372952 (1994). 10 July 2004 <www.ericfacility.net/databases/ERIC_Digests>.

Works Cited

Robinson, Tom. The Everything Science Book. Avon: Adams Media, 2001.

Sawyer, Greg. "Friction and Wear Testing." Tribology Laboratory, the University of Florida. 2004. 22 Sept. 2004.

Schaffner, Don. "Which milk spoils faster, one percent, two percent, whole milk, skim milk?" Food Science, Rutgers University. 2000. 30 April 2005. http://www.madsci.org/posts/archives/jan2000/948927469.Mi.r.html

Scottie. "Traditional Scottish Recipes." 2004. Rampant Scotland. 20 Aug 2004 <www.rampantscotland.com>.

"Vision Conditions." 2004. American Optometric Association. 22 Sept 2004. <www.aoa.org>.